Self-Organizing Men

Conscious Masculinities in Time and Space

EDITED BY
Jay Sennett

HOMOFACTUS PRESS
YPSILANTI

Published in 2006 by
Homofactus Press, L.L.C.
www.homofactuspress.com

About Radicalia Feminista. Phallacies and Queeries: A Phaggot's Contemplations kindly reprinted with permission from the author.

Printed in the United States of America.

ISBN 0-9785973-0-3

Cover art © Eli J. VandenBerg

To Gwyn,
for this and so much more

Table of Contents

Introduction
Jay Sennett

Self-Organizing Men draws its title from the work of Chilean biologists Humberto Maturana and Francisco Varela, who, in 1973, used the term *autopoises* to describe biological systems. Literally meaning auto self-creation, an affinity for the term grew in me. I felt that the term, self-organizing, described my evolution as a transsexual white man. My "self" — that collection of stories I tell about myself in my mind — shifts and changes with input from all my interactions within my chosen worlds.

With new information, my stories about myself have and do change over time. I am always self-organizing and reorganizing. Changing genders is altering both the arc and meaning of my life and providing me with contradictory experiences. I am a man without a penis; a man who used to be a lesbian, girl, female.

These histories and facts did not resolve into neat theories. I transitioned to settle my life, not make it more difficult. A part of me hoped for a place and time where I would stop being sucked further into the vulnerability that exists at the heart of conscious masculinity and conscious living. I wanted to continue to objectify myself as a man the way I had objectified men before hormones.

After starting hormones, I struggled with all the incoming information from my body, family, friends, the world. My opinion suddenly mattered. Women, those humans who most arouse me, flirted more but drew me in less. What was worse is that they had become very, very, very wary of me.

Of course, they would be afraid of me, I told myself at the time: a straight, white dude—everything that was wrong with the world. Despite my work around transsexual activism, sex with women proved to be my Everest. Having sex as a "transsexual man" or "a man who used to be a woman" did not work for me. I wanted to have sex as a man with a woman.

But The Feminist Questions ravaged my psyche: how could I have sex as The Objectifier? Can a woman truly make an consenting decision to sex with a man within patriarchy? If I were straight, how could I be queer? Is all sex between men and women rape?

In early 2002, I began dating the woman who would become my wife. Ms. H. is a very passionate, intelligent woman who, quite simply and by her own admission, "likes fucking guys." Her openness to me as a man — unqualified and unapologetic — astonished me. With her, I felt like the teen-aged boy I had never been, the one who thinks he has discovered sex for the very first time. I fell very hard and fast.

One night we were out at a very crowded club queued up at the bar. I people-watched to pass some time and soon saw a very football-player sized white man about three heads over. If there ever was a man who was The Man, he was it. He had his face turned away from me with his arm around a white woman, a Barbie. I'm sure I thought something mean-spirited in my head: breeder, airhead, dickhead, fill in the blank.

But then he turned back to face the woman and so turned his face to me as well. I still remember the line of his jaw, his softened mouth, relaxed, open face, someone shouting "I'll have two Buds," — Mr. Football Man looked as lovestruck as I felt. Passion and tenderness dripped off his face like melting ice cream. For reasons I still cannot explain, my sense of self radically reorganized in that moment. I became the subject of my life. The passionate hard-on I felt for Ms. H. as a man was mirrored in Mr. Football Man's face. I was him. He was me.

After six years on hormones, I had finally stepped into the center of my masculinity. Sexual love was my rite of manhood.

Since then, I have scoured bookstores looking for books where I might find myself — books that discussed masculine vulnerability, penises, white privilege, living with all of our internal oppositions, childhood, and how to hold all of our paradoxes deep within our hearts.

I didn't find that book, so I decided to create one.

The authors in *Self-Organizing Men* have exceeded my expectations. An anthology is like a jazz-ensemble, and I am thrilled at the concert you have in your hands.

Listen to each author as they describe what conscious masculinity means for them. They may riff off each other or may explore directions that seem out–of–step with the tempo of this book. That is fine. Men — broadly defined to include anyone willing to assume use of the term as meaningful to them — are a varied, contrary lot. I say this mostly for me, since I was the one who tried to goosestep to a kind of bizarre groupthink around notions of purity, and believed I had failed the feminist movement because I had become a man.

I created this book for me, so that I might continue to see myself, or at least try, in the eyes of all men, to continue to say yes to masculinity is all its forms. The authors have each given me a gift, not only through their words, but also for taking a chance on me, a first–time anthologist and publisher.

Self–Organizing Men represents the first book published by Homofactus Press, a collaborative, community–driven publishing company making history one book at a time. I started it because I believe we deserve more than three books a year about our experiences. Others have believed in the merits of this mission as well.

In addition to the authors, I want to thank Jon Allen and Martin Kay and Sheila and Bob King, for their spiritual and financial support. That they are also my parents makes their gifts more serendipitous. I also want to thank Anna Camilleri, for her early and staunch support of my work; Eli Clare, for his vast mind and friendship; Sherrill Morris, for being my very own personal sun; and to Ms. H., for her abiding love, support, and strength of spirit.

Self–Organizing Men has been raised up in an online blogging (web logging) community of evangelists, who have taken time out of their busy lives to review earlier drafts of this book. To Isabella Mori, Kerrick Adrian, Nels P. Highberg, Catherine Chin, Johanna Keller-Fahy, Noah Van Dyke, and Jamie Ward, I offer my gratitude and thanks.

English, like masculinity, is varied and contrary. Rather than attempt to quell the living entity that is the English language, I have chosen to keep spelling and slang variations in the texts that follow. With authors from Australia, Canada, Great Britain, and the United States, you may get some sense of how varied English really is.

After reading this book, should you have something you want to share with us, a conversation you need to have, or just general feedback, we look forward to conversing with you at www.homofactuspress.com.

Better Branding Opportunities

Jay Sennett

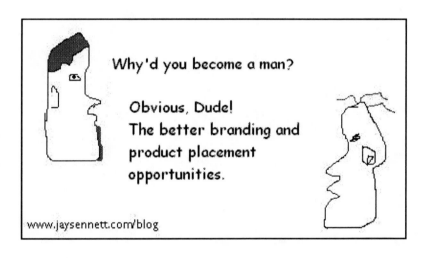

More Masculinities, More of the Time

Aren Z. Aizura

One: Envy

At times I am a man. I don't have a penis.
I am not a man. But often I have a penis.

I'm walking down the street in summer. It could be
any street, any city, any version of summer: sweaty,
sweltering monsoon, or dry windy heat. As I walk,
I'm calculating the passability of my moving body.
How masculine is my walk today? Are my buttocks
tucked under, concealing the tell–tale femininity of
their curves? Are my hips swinging, or am I "leading
from the shoulders," as so many FtM passing tip sites
assure me that all men do? Am I emanating broad-
ness, a comfortable ownership of the space around
me?

I try not to check my reflection in the shop windows, but the temptation is great. I'm sneaking a look at my bum in the window of a Chinese grocery when a young man walks past me with a rolling, easy gait. He's wearing a t–shirt and shorts, the same as me, but he manages to fit his clothes in a way I only wish I could. His long pale legs support two neat butt cheeks. A slim waist broadens out to narrow but strong–looking shoulders. He has a little beer gut, probably doesn't go to the gym, and he could do with a shave. But he's fucking beautiful. It's there in his stride: the way his sandalled feet slide across the con-crete, the way his eyes sweep the street like he owns it, the way he holds himself. He's in his body.

I am wearing exactly the same semi–uniform: shorts, t–shirt, and sandals. I am also young, and I identify as male. But looking at him fills me with envy. He never had to want that body. It was given to him. He never had to fight the distribution of fat around his hips and thighs and stomach that would wrongly code him as female; he never had to inject hormones to make his beard grow; he never had to worry that he was anything but what he is: equipped with a penis and, therefore, male. Deep down I know that, of course, he can't have such an uncomplicated rela-tionship with his body. He probably thinks he's fat, or maybe his girlfriend hassles him about getting more exercise. Maybe he has pimples on his back or a small penis. But it's likely that he has a penis. This is the one thing that pretty much all men have. And it's the one thing I don't.

Well, I do, sometimes. Have a cock, I mean. Any trans man will tell you that he certainly has a cock, maybe more than one, and he'd be rightly offended if you told him he didn't. Much of the extant writing about sex from a trans masculine perspective has detailed the numerous ways in which a FtM or a tranny boy can fuck with a cock. Use your imagination. Silicon, rubber, penis pumping, metoidioplasty, phalloplasty: these are the usual options listed. And these options work well, mostly. But sometimes it seems as if there's a little pressure to declaim, loudly, the pleasures and the advantages of having that kind of cock and a side–stepping of the angst and difficulty and plain, crappy, despairing envy that comes with being born not–female in a manifestly female body. For me, at least, the notion of "having a cock" also describes a lack, a wish, an impossibility. No matter how hard you pray (or save), you can't surgically attach a fully functioning penis, complete with testes, scrotum, urethra, ejaculate, and sperm. You can get something that may look a lot like a dick and that may approximate some of its "natural" functions. But, as the saying goes, you generally can't make a surgically constructed urinating penis sensitive to sexual stimulation, and you generally can't make a sexually "functional" surgically constructed penis to urinate through. The word "functional" here is used loosely, and whatever the dick, it will cost tens of thousands of dollars. So, I feel envy: not only for those people born with bodies that look and feel and smell "male" but for the genitals that mark and reproduce our ideas about gender.

Rationally, though, I don't believe in indulging envy of any kind. I don't believe that masculinity equals a penis, just as I don't believe that sex means "hide the penis in the lady."[1] I desire freedom not only physically, from the prison of my gendered body, but politically. That means freedom from the rules of "gendered realness" that say a man is not a man without a penis, and a woman is not a woman without a vagina. The rules governing trans realness constrict choices: choices about how we should look and behave (like stereotypical examples of one gender or the other, apparently) and what pronouns we should use (the ones that most people would use if meeting us for the first time). The rules also dictate whether gender transgressive people must pass as "real" men and women in order to be accepted or free of violence.

Now, it seems obvious to me that gender is fluid and multiple. Years of reading feminist theory have given me the tools to deconstruct that ideology of gendered realness. Years of reading wacky French philosophers have also furnished me with the knowledge that no body is perfectly gendered as entirely male or entirely female. Nobody operates purely on a psychoanalytic plane where sexual difference — the possession or lack of a phallus — is the only game in town. In Spinoza's words, "We still don't know what a body can do." Therefore, masculinity has to be multiple, too. Any thing, any body, any shape, any arrangement of genitals, in the right light, could be masculine. According to this logic, my body, my genitals, my mannerisms are already masculine. They shouldn't depend on the presence of a "real" dick to count.

But my yearnings and my shame at not having what I feel I should have make me wary of dispatching the desire for a cock as part of a suspect project to turn me into a real man. No matter what happens on the level of thought, the physical experience of yearning remains. I don't always experience the close, crude, and unshakably deep desire to have a flesh penis. Sometimes it goes somewhere else for a while, not absent entirely, just distant. But the desire is present more often than not. When it arrives, it stays with me for months. I "feel" a penis, balls, the whole deal — like a phantom limb. Just here — but never really here. My sexual fantasies become centred exclusively on how a "real" penis would feel, how it would smell, how I would come. Real sex becomes burdened with my shame at not having that which I feel I need. I also get a little depressed. After all, it's a hopeless case. There is no solution to this problem.

Like a depression, I make attempts to shake it off, this desire. I try to avoid it, ignore it, distract myself. I rarely travel into the feeling, observing, taking notes, asking questions. If masculinity is not about penises, then how come I want one so badly?

This essay is the result of my attempt to turn out the internal architecture of my yearning. I would be lying if I said it was easy to write: it hasn't been. On the other hand, writing this has opened up new questions and an opportunity for reinvention. If masculinity can be multiple, centred not on the possession of a real cock (or even a "symbolic" phallus in the form of male privilege, logic, rationality, the all–seeing eye), what does that multiplicity look like? What are its sensory repertories? What does it smell like, taste like? What are its modes of becoming? How can I study them?

Two: Size Queen

Let's start with what I've got. I've about three silicon or plastic dicks, a couple of harnesses, a testosterone–enhanced lump of "FtM–specific erogenous tissue,"[2] and the persistent feeling that a flesh penis, attached to me, complete with balls, foreskin, veiny bits, and the tendency to stiffen uncontrollably, might magically unfold from my groin if someone pushed the right button. On occasion, I experience a sensation akin to what might happen if someone pushed that button. It feels intensely right—for as long as I can sustain suspension of disbelief.

There are other methods.

I'm by myself, and it's late. My lover is away. As much as I wish she was here, this night is set aside for solo research. Since I began taking testosterone three years ago, masturbation has become a necessity and a pleasure. I was never really into it before. Now, as well as letting off steam, masturbating helps me figure out how to deal with this changing and unpredictable thing, my sexed body. While the bits changed shape, sensation, feeling, intensity, I had to learn all over again how to get off. Wanking is also a research project into how to make my dick more like a dick. I could do this with my lover, and sometimes I do. But after three years of transition–related self–absorption, I am wary of making our sexual life just about my dick. And part of me cannot bear the thought of spreading my legs for her to watch or participate in this. It's too instrumentalised, too experimental.

I've propped myself up on pillows in bed with my knees up and the blankets shoved around my ankles. Beside me on the bed are lube, a silver thumb ring, and a length of stretchy black spaghetti strap with an adjustable noose at one end, which I cut from a shirt my lover bought and never wore. It's tiny like a doll's bra strap. In this business, small is beautiful. With one hand I pull my pubic hair up to get it out of the way. With the other hand, I take the strap and slip the noose over the head of my cock, flicking and pinching it a little to get it hard. My cock is about half an inch "wide" and one inch "long" flaccid, although there is no defined point where my labia end and the cock starts, and anyhow, who cares? (I do.) It's as if I have the circumcised head of a "real" cock attached to my groin without any length of muscle. Once the noose is resting at the base, as far down as I can secure it, I pull the noose tight. Tightening is painful and slow, since it's easy for pubic hairs to catch in the loop. When I pull the noose tight enough, it sits snug under a kind of ridge, a seam that differentiates the bundle of nerves in the "head" from the skin and thinner nerves constituting the "length." As I plan, the noose traps blood on the "head," producing a bigger erection.

How erect is your penis?
What are you thinking about?
What does your penis look like?
How does this feel?
How easy would it be to come right now?

Lest you think this is all in the service of pervy bondage play, I am also trying to be methodical. I check the tightness of the restraint, note the colour and the amount of swelling and sensation, note how much tightening hurts and how the pain wears off after I stop pulling the loop tighter. My cock protrudes. It reminds me of my smallest left toe, a swollen, sunburnt paean to cheap shoes. I feel slight nicks of pain where the metal adjuster digs into the flesh. In the past, I've stopped at this point and played with the cock as it is. I've tried stretching the strap up or down, close to my body or away from it, tried pulling tight and letting go, holding the end of the strap in my teeth while I touch it, rub it with various substances, and even, once, made an interconnected web of pleasurable discomfort by attaching the strap to nipple clamps. This time, I have other ideas.

With the length of black strap remaining, about twelve inches, I wrap up my cock. The strap makes neat loops, not tight enough to cut off circulation, but enough, again, to retain more blood in the head. I wrap closer to the base, stretching the length of the tissue and using the loops of the strap to make a stiffer, harder, more jutting thing. I fold the end of the strap underneath the wrappings, as neatly as it will go, hoping it doesn't come loose. Finally, I push the thumb ring over the head of my cock, over the wrapped cord, over the original loop (with some difficulty, as the strap has thickened and stiffened the circumference of the flesh). Pushed as far down as it will go, the ring wedges itself between my pubic bone and the wrappings, stretching the fold of skin and providing a solid prosthetic base. It feels odd to say "everything." We're talking about nothing larger than the width and length of my thumb here. But that's pretty much "everything."

My cock—this prosthetic device—is now ready for action. A palm could encircle its girth. If it were wrapped in latex to smooth the friction of the nylon strap and the metal of the ring, it could penetrate someone or something. Someone could suck it. Most of all, the head is exposed: constricted and blood-filled, sensitive like pins and needles, but exposed, hard, "erect."

But once I'm here, trussed up like a miniature lamb roast, I'm don't know what comes next. I rub it inside my palm. I touch the head and think about the size of the mouth it would fill. It's an obscene and discomforting thought. It occurs to me that although I've been scientific with my method, my research objectives need development. Why am I doing this? What happens now? I've been trying to reassemble the fleshy parts of my genitals into a different configuration that respond and behave differently. I've been trying to make my dick more like a dick. Is it about finding a new way to reach orgasm? Now that I have something that approximates the shape, however oddly, of a functioning human penis, what have I learnt?

I learn that it is possible. I also learn that the mundane reality — the cool instrumental rationality with which I regard myself during this exercise — eventually kills off pleasure. It becomes about nuts and bolts, architecture rather than feeling. Up this alley of possible difference, shape and size are too important, too foregrounded, to ignore. I also learn that taking the ring and the knots off afterwards really hurts. There, in that pain, the pain of undoing, lies my chance for getting off. Blood rushes back into my constricted cock, and the pain makes me light-headed. Was it all for this? I can't come trussed up. In the endorphin rush of the unwrapping, I slather lube on and rub myself to an orgasm. At least I come like a guy: short, sharp, violent, and effortlessly sleepy afterwards.

Three: The Growth

A hospital. A dream hospital, in which the Casualty Department is empty, and nobody screams at anyone else. No bloody faces, no rowing couples, no vomiting children. Just me, my lover A., and two duty nurses, who do not ask me to fill in any forms. When we approach the desk, a woman in her thirties with glitter nail polish looks up from her paperwork with a sunny smile and says, "What's the problem, dear?"

"I have a... There's a growth," I say. "A growth in my genital area."

"Does it look sort of cauliflower–like? White? Or is it more pussy and weeping?"

"It's not a sore. I mean, it's not diseased. It just wasn't there before," I say. "It's sort of... full grown. And yesterday it didn't exist."

She catches herself before her smile flattens into a smirk. "I see. Well, we'll just call someone and see what we can do." She punches a number into the phone. Presently, a muffled voice answers and she says, "Eric. Sandra from Casualty. One for you, I'm afraid. What? Some kind of 'growth.' Says it wasn't there yesterday. Okay. Thanks." She hangs up, and her smile is dazzling.

"Dr. Eric will see you shortly."

They give me a paper robe to wear, with tiny pin-holes imprinted in the crepe and a large gap at the rear, revealing, I assume, the pimples on my back. I squeeze my lover's hand. They make her wait outside, although there's a glass window through which she can watch the proceedings. Sandra asks me to lie on a steel gurney with more crepe paper underneath; it crackles when I lie down. There's a bright light above, one of those heat lights that are usually used in bathrooms. I feel my pores opening under it.

The warmth makes it stiffen. It's a good size, long enough to brush a freckle on my inner left thigh, five inches below the pelvic crease. It's pale, uncircumcised, and quite clean. Hangs to the left. The balls, now, they're sublime. Before I woke A. this morning to tell her, before the question of hospital had even come up, I hid in the bathroom and held them in my hands, to understand their weight, to feel the firm inner teste roll inside its babysmooth pouch of skin, to let the balls fall free and allow their weight to stretch the skin, the skin on the top layer stretching the lower skin on my stomach, the underside of the scrotal sac sliding against my perineum. Velvety.

That's the weird thing about cocks, the thing they never tell you: the softness of the skin.

Even though I've had it less than a day, I could catalogue the sensations. The way it feels to hold the foreskin gently between finger and thumb and slide it back, revealing a glans the colour of bruised, mottled fuschia. You can see tiny veins. A larger vein. It's not fat, but rather thin — and now it swells in the gloved hands of Sandra from Casualty.

She picks it up, rolls back the foreskin, stretches it out like it's made of rubber. It hurts. She releases it then, and my cock grows more, waving slightly like an antennae, unstable. It juts. I take in how it is to jut. Blood rushes to the surface of my cheeks. Sandra pretends not to notice.

Meanwhile, Dr. Eric smiles, holding his clipboard, writing with his blue Bic pen. I try to meet A.'s eyes through the window. Her eyebrows are raised, but she's smiling. I smile back. Her mouth moves; words form. I think I recognise the word "perv."

"Now Aren, you say this simply wasn't here yesterday?" Dr. Eric asks me.

"I was — am, transgendered. I was born a woman, with a vagina. I've been taking testosterone for a few years now. But this just seemed to be there when I woke up this morning."

Dr. Eric doesn't seem fazed by what I'm telling him. Actually, no one in this dream seems fazed by my new dick. This is partially how I know it's a dream. You'd have thought even A. would be a little surprised, but when I finally let her into the bathroom in the morning and let her remove the towel I'd wrapped around my hips to hide the evidence, she was strangely serene.

Dr. Eric uses the time–honoured bedside technique of saying my name often, to reassure me. Like all doctors, he pronounces it wrong.

"Well, this doesn't happen too often, Aren. There are a series of tests we'd like to perform, just to make sure everything's functional and working properly. We'd like to take down your details, and later we'll read some phrases to you and gauge a response. Now Aren," Dr. Eric raises his eyebrows and looks me in the eye, "some of these things may be of a sexual nature, and I don't want you to be embarrassed about any response you may have. Arousal is perfectly normal under these circumstances."

First, of course, questions about my sexual and gendered history. Sexual orientation. Hormones I've been on. Psychologists I've seen. Later, they ask me to urinate into a glass jar. They ask if I've always urinated standing up, and I say no. I wonder how my peeing style could possibly relate to growing a penis. They tap my knees with a hammer, examine my ears, my eyes, my throat. They ask about histories of heart disease, cancer, and any vaccinations I've had recently. They examine the penis itself: taking photographs; measuring its length, width, and diameter; checking under the foreskin (which I'm pleased to say is very clean); and palpating the testes.

Then the psychological testing begins. Dr. Eric and Sandra produce a small booklet with a greyish–green cover. They read aloud. "Think of a woman with large breasts. Think of burying your face in them and licking the nipples," says Sandra with emphatic tonelessness. That does exactly nothing. Dr. Eric makes a note on his clipboard. Another one. "Imagine you're on your knees," she reads, chuckling now. "You are fellating a man with an enormous cock, and you cannot quite fit it into your mouth." They seem preoccupied with oversize scenarios. Dr. Eric reads next, slowly and carefully as if from a schoolbook, a long passage: "Think of a woman lying on a bed facing you. Think of lying on top of her and inserting yourself in her vagina. Think of moving inside her and coming out, think of thrusting. Think of the tightness. Think of her eyes open and watching you. Think of her hands gripping your hair. Pulling it. Think of her scratching your back with her hands." Again, nothing. Dr. Eric scribbles. Now Sandra flips to a random page and reads, "A nurse with large bosoms and a huge thermometer…" She stops there, grimacing. "Why don't we skip that one."

They read out story after story, each one involving a more convoluted set of activities. The stories are like the porn you'd find in an airport bookshop, banal and asensual. But it doesn't seem to matter. With each additional sentence, I begin to feel my temperature rising. My cheeks flush. The heat spreads to the base of my stomach, and then I'm getting hard. I try to fight it, to think really unsexy thoughts: the dishes, putting out the rubbish, the way the bin smelt the time we threw out a bag of liver scraps from making pâté and the rats pierced the bag. It doesn't stop. Dr.

Eric and Sandra keep reading aloud, no longer pausing to make notes. I close my eyes, half wanting it to be over and half enjoying the attention. If I only have this dick for a day, I realise, I'm going to have spent at least three hours in hospital when I could have been fucking, donating sperm to dyke friends trying to get pregnant, or urinating standing up.

They're touching my cock again. Pulling at it. They instruct me to hold on as long as I can. My balls tighten. They ask me to slide my feet up, knees bent, so that my rectum is exposed. "Now raise your legs for me, dear," Sandra says. She produces a white rod, about half an inch wide and ten inches long. She squirts clear lubricant onto her gloved right index finger and massages my asshole. Dr. Eric tells me to take a breath. Sandra inserts the rod. It goes in deep. They instruct me to hold it there. I try to hold the rod in. They tap it. They hold it at the far end and tap it right up near my hole, and the tapping makes me shiver and moan.

"Aren, we just want to know one last thing," Dr. Eric says. "We'd like to know whether you've grown a prostate gland. Now, you may have heard that male ejaculation can be caused by a physiological response to stimulation of the prostate. We'll be able to tell by this simple procedure." Sandra begins to fuck me with the rod. She pulls it out and pushes it back in — fast after a pause, a jolted, jerky rhythm — deep inside me. The rod connects to a nerve or zone behind my ass. Precome drips down my glans. I feel it oozing out, and it's warm and then cold, and it makes me gasp. With every thrust I feel my balls tightening and my cock jerking, waving, flexing. Finally she rams the rod in very hard and very fast, three times, and on the third thrust I ejaculate. Spurts of come glob onto my lower abdomen.

Sandra throws the rod into a yellow bin marked "Toxic Waste." She washes her hands. She swabs at the come on my belly with a cotton bud and scrapes some of it onto a petri dish, closes it, labels it with a red texta. I suppress the desire to roll over and curl into a post–orgasmic ball. She hands me a medicated towelette to wipe myself off: cool, stinging alcohol. "There you go," she says. "You can get dressed." She draws the curtain and leaves the room. She stops by A. on the way out, and through the curtain I see them laughing together. When I open the curtain again, Dr. Eric is writing on his clipboard. He signs something at the bottom with a flourish.

"Well, Aren, that's settled. This doesn't happen often, but it seems that you've grown a penis. That penis is anatomically consistent and appears in full working order. We've taken a swab for analysis, of course; it would be unlikely that the fluid has live sperm in it, but one never knows. I'd like you to come back in a month just to make sure everything's progressing well. Just remember," he says, "always use protection." And he winks, "No matter who's fucking you."

On the bus trip home, A. and I grip hands sweatily and say little. She presses her thumb into the back of my hand, the only indication of how fierce she's feeling. Finally, I turn to her. "Well? What do you want to do with it?"

She doesn't answer me until we get home. After closing the front door and dropping her bag on the ground, she pulls me into the bedroom, strips me, ties me to the bed, and plunges her lubed hand into my bonus tranny hole.[3] "Wank for me, boy," she says. "Wank for me while I fist you." And I do.

Four: Against An Envy Economy

It's no secret that a lot of lesbians have learnt about sex from gay men. If sexual historians like Gayle Rubin are correct, fisting began as anal play in gay SM bars in the 1970s and only became a widespread lesbian practice, as vaginal fisting, afterwards.[4] As David Halperin has argued, fist–fucking (with its extended temporality, its direction towards pleasure rather than orgasm) can be seen as a refusal of the assumption that "sexual pleasure is at the root of all our possible pleasures."[5] But it also works as a refusal of the idea that sex means vaginal penetration with a penis. If pleasure is to come from any zone of the body (and from any kind of sensation: pain, itching, heat, cold, restraint, sensory deprivation, et al.), the penis loses both its central relevance to defining the sex act and its symbolic importance as the object whose presence or lack allegedly inscribes and constructs Western gendered subjectivity.

It is no secret, either, that many Euro–American trans men, FtMs, and masculine genderqueers are fascinated by, and drawn to, gay male sex culture (sometimes circulated through dyke cultures, too). This interest, for me, is as much in the shifting gendered possibilities of Daddy–boy play, in which new boys may learn from scratch how to be men,[6] as by the tradition of worshipping cock, of casual anonymous sex, of brief, explosive encounters. This iconography of queer sex also works as a solution to the problem of retaining queerness some trans men and boys have when they become nominally "straight men" after having identified as lesbians. Queerness drifts from same–sex encounters in the context of lesbianism to same–sex encounters in the context of gayness.

The "dream" sequence above is my attempt to queer and rewire a stereotypical heteroporn nurse fantasy and the fantasy of "a dick for a day," by making anal penetration the ultimate road test of the protagonist's new penis. Masculine sexuality here is defined not by the capacity to behave dominantly nor to put one's pole in a hole. It's defined by a queer anatomical coincidence: the fact that stimulation of the prostate gland sends most people with prostate glands wild. Masculinity is also about the ability to take it lying down, to submit, to turn embarrassment into pleasure, and finally, to multiply the possible sites of pleasure, rather than substituting one for the other.

Material FtM involvement in gay sex culture is seductive and fun. For some people it's the way they've always done it. But it can also be another kind of fantasy. To begin with, there are the troubles some gay men have accepting trans men as men, when there's such a premium on what is hypocritically called "the real thing." Secondly, a tension erupts, particularly for trans men who have been or are in relationships with women through transition. On a recent episode of the TV series *The L Word*, Max, a FtM, wants to fuck queer men because "it makes [him] feel more like a guy." Meanwhile, his long–suffering girlfriend takes on the task of caring for him emotionally. It seems that for Max, fucking a guy with a silicon cock is easier than negotiating the uneasy, difficult terrain between "lesbian" and "straight" (or somewhere queerer than that, maybe) that erupts with his female partner. Caught between lesbian butchness and heterosexual manhood, Max opts momentarily to be queer somehow else. In the process, he acts like an asshole.

Many trans viewers of *The L Word* decided the writers were being transphobic in their portrayal of this character: a petition was circulated demanding that the writers portray their trans characters in a more positive light. And no, the character is neither sympathetic nor a positive representation of transness.[7] But I would be lying if I didn't admit to sometimes feeling

exactly the same way as Max. If I have merely fanta-
sised my transgressions, but Max acts his out, does
that make me better than him? Ultimately, assuming
queer male–to–male sex will solve the difficulties of
fucking someone with the "same" plumbing as you is
a chimera.

The solution to all of these problems lies not in fucking the people who reflect back one's fantasies, but to
respect and take joy in the unique configuration of
desires in every person we encounter sexually — no
matter what genders they might be. It means stepping out of angst–ridden self–absorption and observing the manifold difficulties of having genitals in the
first place. Everyone experiences fraught and complex sexual and gender identifications, whether they
identify as trans or not. Masculinity is fraught for all
men, with and without penises, those with large
dicks and those with small, those with penises that
hang to the left and that bend in the middle, those
that refuse to get hard when they should and those
that won't stop being hard. These multiple ways of
having a penis produce multiple "masculinities"
already, even without the addition of trans masculinities to the fold. So, how can trans masculinities contribute (even more than they already do) to the
multiplication, the broadening out, of masculinity
itself?

Though it should be a given, it's important to point
out here that race, class, language, and geographic
location (among other things) contribute to the multi-

plication of trans sexual cultures and masculinities, and masculinities generally. One factor prime for multiplication (and decentering) is racialisation: particularly the mostly white racial markings of prosthetic dicks for sale in an increasingly consumerist "FtM accessory" market. There may be many skin shades available, but the majority of demo photographs on prosthetic dick websites are pink.[8]

But this multiplicity of masculinities I am arguing for here is not about the liberal multiplication of choice for the purposes of consumption, of sex toys, surgeries, or anything else. In reality, those who are non-white are often also poor. Poor people cannot afford to buy non-white prosthetic dicks on the internet, let alone get an approval for a credit card. They may not even be able to afford gender reassignment surgeries. Recently, I have been travelling in Thailand, where tom-dee couples (a Thai equivalent to butch/FtM-femme) are visible and numerous. Gender reassignment clinics are also numerous here: despite the fact that most surgeons cater to trans women, some surgeons also offer chest reconstruction, metoidioplasty, and phalloplasty. Yet on a large Yahoo group for Asian trans men, there seem to be no Thais.

This email list functions as a source of information about Thai surgeons for generally middle-class Asian trans men in Singapore, Malaysia, Hong Kong, Australia, and the United States, but it does not seem to interface at all with Thai trans masculine culture.

Megan Sinnott, an anthropologist and the author of *Toms and Dees: Transgender Identity and Female Same-Sex Relationships in Thailand,* states that she has only ever met one Thai tom who wanted to live as a man. Aside from other factors, a possible explanation might be that in Thailand, even "middle-class" affluence might not make it possible to afford the cost of gender reconstruction surgery — even without travel expenses.[9] The Thai tom-dee website Lesla (www.lesla.com) prominently features chest binding instructions, but no surgeon information. This situation exemplifies the uneven distribution of FtM surgeries and accessories across language, nation, and region as they intersect with global capitalism.

Capitalism tells us that everything in the world, even feelings, work on a scarcity model: that we have to hoard our pleasures and our identities and disavow those who might trouble or complicate them, that we have to "save up" to money and moral worth to deserve the good things that come our way. It makes us work for crappy pay, and then it makes us believe we are nothing without the latest gadget. Or is that the other way around? Sometime this century, stem cell research will enable lab technicians to grow penises in test tubes. Capitalism dictates that if we save up very hard, and maybe have a mansion on hand to refinance, we will be able to pay for that pleasure.

I'm not sure what to do about this feeling of yearning that is still lurking in my body. It may not ever leave:

maybe I'm stuck with it, stuck with wanting, stuck with "lack." But I do know that designing my life around external "relief" of any kind doesn't work, whether it's waiting for the test–tube cock or buying a roomful of sex toys to mask what I don't have. I know that instead of shame, I should feel proud: proud of managing, somehow, proud of what I do have. I know that letting the yearning become bitter and covetous, rather than merely sad, takes away my power to pleasure myself, to believe I can take pleasure. I do not want to be like some trans men who refuse all sexual encounters point blank until they can access phalloplasty. For no pleasure, not even for people who have penises and vaginas they are entirely happy with, can ever be totally "whole" or "right." Pleasure is always momentary, fractured, ambivalent. You have to take it while you have the chance. The rest of the time, you have to think about ways to multiply the opportunities where pleasure might hit its mark. Next time I walk past a boy and I become aware of our differences, maybe I'll be glad that he's him, and I'm me.

Notes

1. I'm grateful to commenter alas, on www.Barbelith.com, for this most excellent descriptor.

2. The phrase "FtM specific erogenous tissue" was coined by Jacob Hale.

3. "Bonus tranny hole" is Dean Spade's invented term for what tranny boys and trans men prefer to call a "vagina." See Dean Spade, on *Makezine* (http://www.makezine.org/january02.html).

4. Gayle Rubin, "The Catacombs: A Temple of the Butthole" in Mark Thompson, *Leatherfolk: Radical Sex, People, Politics and Practice* (Boston: Alyson, 1991): 119-41.

5. David Halperin, quoting Michel Foucault in a French language inteview with Madeleine Champsal, in *Saint Foucault: Towards A Gay Hagiography* (Oxford: Oxford University Press, 1995): 91.

6. For an exciting and personal exploration of Daddy–boy play as it relates to transgendered manhood, see Jacob Hale, "Leatherdyke Boys and Their Daddies: How to Have Sex Without Women or Men," *Social Text* 52-53 (1996): 223-236.

7. The criticisms put by the petition also included inaccurate and misleading representations of trans healthcare: Max procures his testosterone on the black market and is never asked to see a psychiatrist, even when he consults a surgeon for chest reconstruction. This may be the situation for affluent FtMs in Los Angeles (where *The L Word* is set) but it is not the case all over the United States. A

lengthy debate circulated online after the screening of these episodes about whether *The L Word* has a political responsibility to represent its trans characters accurately or positively, and a simultaneous (but perhaps more important) debate about the representation of non–white characters. See http://feministe.us/blog/; http://www.petitionspot.com/petitions/lwordistransphobic; http://goingsomewhere.blogsome.com/; http://www.jaysennett.com/blog.

8. One notable exception is www.djknowsdicks.com, whose demonstration photographs on how to use the Pissin' Passin' Packer present a model proudly demo'ing the CinnaMAN Brown version.

9. There are many other factors which may come into play, however, and I am not able to offer a comprehensive account of them here. It may be that since the Thai tom–dee community is so large, and since surgeons are easily accessible, anyone desiring FtM gender reassignment surgery would not need to consult an English language email list. For more reading, see Megan Sinnott, *Toms and Dees: Transgender and Female Same-Sex Relationships in Thailand* (Honolulu: University of Hawaii Press, 2004); also Ara Wilson, "The Intimate Economies of Bangkok: Tomboys, Tycoons and Avon Ladies" *The Global City* (Berkeley: University of California, 2004); and Peter Jackson and Nerida Cook (eds), *Gender and Sexualities in Modern Thailand* (Chiang Mai: Silkworm Books, 1999).

Body in Progress
Eli J. VandenBerg

I guess you could call it penis envy.
ink on paper

"Well, you're always going to have trouble," he said. I nodded, knowing I probably was a difficult size. "You're never going to find something right off the rack," he continued. "Maybe you could try a children's store and see if they have a 'husky boys' department." I nodded and hoped he'd realize that what I was really saying was your help is the biggest slap to my self–esteem that I've experienced since elementary school. He didn't stop. "I mean, you could try a big and tall shop, but you're not tall, just big." That's when it finally hit me. I was no longer experiencing the soft pat on the shoulder that a woman gets while shopping. I was getting the honest truth. I was short, I was big, and I was going to have trouble finding a suit that fit. Although you'd never hear a salesman telling a woman, "I'm sorry but you're just too short and fat for all the clothing in this store," to tell me essentially the same thing was perfectly acceptable. I looked up at him as he handed me his card and thanked him for his time and honesty, man to man.

**The problem always seems
bigger than it really is.**
woodcut

I decided to start hormone replacement therapy in June of 2004. When I began seeing her I told her that within the next year I wanted to have top surgery, and on January 11, 2005, I went down to Baltimore for chest reconstruction surgery. Something that the year before was just a dream I never believed could be a reality had actually come true. I woke up in the recovery room and looked down at my body. I looked normal for the first time.

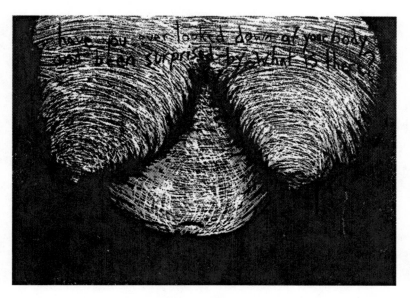

**Have you ever looked down at your body and
been surprised by what is there?**
woodcut and mixed media

We then left the office, a bit shocked, to take my breasts on their last outings. I had my last trip to the bookstore with boobs, my last trip to the aquarium with boobs, my last dinner with boobs, and my last time getting drunk with boobs. We all went back to the hotel room that night sensing the gravity of the next day, but buzzed enough to not really talk about it. I went to sleep terrified, but I wasn't about to admit that to anyone. I knew they were probably just as scared as I was.

In memoriam.
woodcut

I decided that when I moved to New York I would become a man. Literally. For the first time since college I would be entering an entirely new world with new social contacts, and I wanted this transition to be immediate. I wanted to bind my breasts, call myself by a boy's name, and everyone could just assume that I was what I claimed to be. The problem was registration was a warm day in August—not a day to begin regular breast binding—and, of course, I enrolled under the name Elizabeth. I was standing on the steps. One of my new classmates asked me my name. Betsy rolled off my tongue before I could stop myself. I went home feeling defeated, but this was a self-prescribed defeat.

I wasn't ready.

I wasn't physically ready to safely walk through life as a man. I wasn't mentally ready to defend my chosen gender. I wasn't emotionally ready to deal with those who questioned my manhood, and most importantly, I wasn't spiritually ready to stop feeling apologetic for living out my true self. I had to learn to stop feeling like it was my fault that I was challenging others to stretch their minds around gender beyond what they understood it to be.

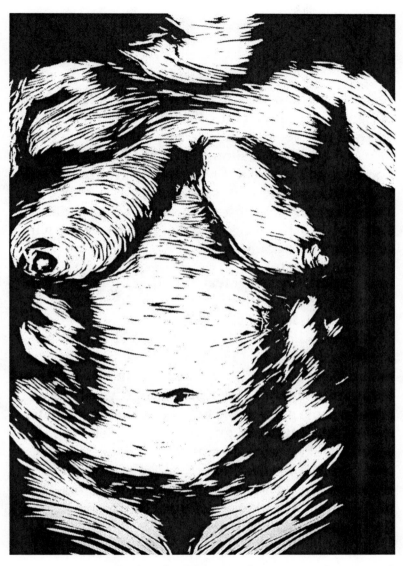

**His body was easier to understand
when he didn't look at his face.**
woodcut

I have never had to hit the dating scene in this newly designed masculine body. I've never had to enter a room of people and, upon seeing a person of interest, face that intense question, "Does she know, and if not, how and when do I tell her?" I have traditionally been one to paralyze myself with worry. I worry about standing too close to someone or too far away. I am overly self-conscious about the size of my hands or my lack of Adam's apple.

In my mind, my worst fear isn't that I'd merely surprise a potential partner and that she'd exclaim, "Really, you used to be a woman? I never would have guessed." Rather, I fear that she'd run screaming from the room and lock herself in the bathroom where she'd begin frantically calling her ex-boyfriend because she needs to hear the voice of a real man. I'd later be some story she'd tell over a dinner party to excited and entranced guests as the day she experienced a real life crying game, or I'd be destined to come up in some desperate therapy session where she recounts her attraction to me and wonders if underlying lesbian tendencies are the reason she can't find a good man.

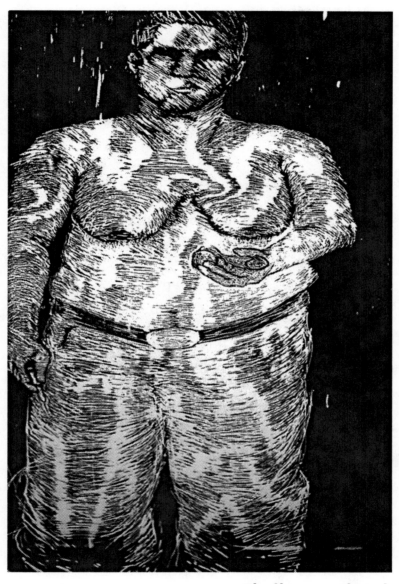

Finding manhood.
woodcut

After a few minutes, he emerged from the bathroom angry and dejected. He stormed over to his stool, where he grabbed his coat, and moved swiftly to the door, but paused in front of me to glare directly into my eyes.

Then I finally caught on. I was the one he was after. I was the one he wanted to do in the bathroom. As he stormed out the door, a wave of excitement passed over me. I was the one he was looking at. I was the man he wanted for the night. Not only did this drunken stranger see me as a man, he saw me as a man he wanted to fuck. This drunken lust of a gay man did wonders for my self-confidence, far more than a year of therapy ever could.

Untitled.
lithograph

Before Dad left my apartment, I asked for a picture of his chest. I was looking into different plastic surgeons for my chest reconstruction surgery. I wanted my nipples to look like I had been born his son. He looked at me and said, "Honey, I love you, but that's a little too weird for me, to think that I might look at you with your shirt off and think, 'that's where my nipples are,' but I'll think about it." That's all I was asking for.

In November, we were sitting around the Thanksgiving dinner table. He turned to me, patted my hand and said, "Honey, it's still a little weird for me, but if you want a picture of my nipples you can have that." I was amused, but even more touched by his love for me.

In December, I asked my mom if she could take the picture of my dad's chest. I knew he was still a bit uncomfortable. I didn't want to push him. She arrived in January, two days before my surgery and told me he just couldn't do it. "He tried, he really did, but it was just too weird for him." I smiled and told her I knew it would be and that it was okay. I was willing to leave my nipples up to fate.

After all, that's what you do when you have a son. His body is out of their hands. My chest was out of mine.

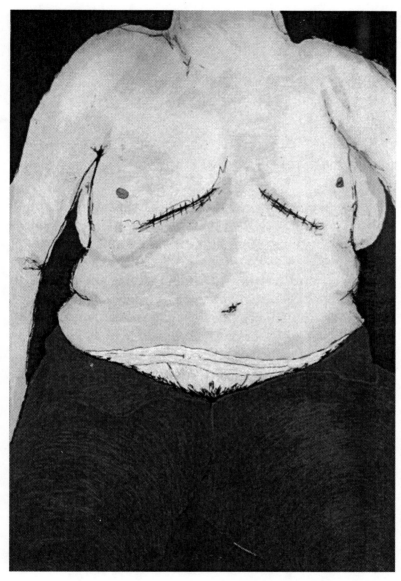

Self-portrait seated.
silkscreen

Like any teenage boy, I think about sex. A lot. Lying in bed at night, I'll flash back to seeing my girlfriend naked after getting out of the shower that morning. I'll feel a surge between my legs. My mind will begin to wonder and wander to fantasies like: was I born with a dick? Did I already have surgery? Is my body as it looks now? Does she find my transsexuality hot and we have wild, crazy, queer sex, or was I actually born into the male body I've always imagined? I'll usually settle on a real, live functioning penis seeing as my fantasies are the only place I actually get to have one.

The male gaze, even mine, seemed to make her nervous.

**The male gaze, even mine, seemed
to make her nervous.**
ink on paper

Are We There Yet?
Scott Turner Schofield

Would you believe I was almost homecoming queen
in high school?

Picture it:
football field, fluorescent light
Miss Congeniality on one side
Miss Best Dressed on the other
and me.

Blank stares, nervous laughter —
I gotta tell you some things
You gotta know
where I'm coming from
to fully grasp the
horrifying nightmare of this night.

—Excerpt from *Underground Transit*

Until about three months ago, I would speak these opening lines of my first solo performance art effort, *Underground Transit*, and most audience members would smile at the visual gag of the introduction: a clearly queer, but obviously female actor standing before them. They would come along for the ride. Nearly everyone could believe the queer reality of that iconic high school moment as I describe it in the performance; no matter how masculine I appeared, even while sporting a skirt and tiny–T at the top of the show, my woman's voice reassured anyone watching of the probable truth of my autobiographical story. Then, my voice changed.

I became a transgender performance artist because I am a gender–transgressive actor and writer who could not find work in mainstream theater. What's more, I am a transgender, feminist theater lover who yearns, always, for greater diversity in the stories that are told on stage: mine and stories like it represent just one part of the bigger picture most audiences will never see. Rather than wait for the perfect role to come along, in 2000, I began to write a script for myself, my sexuality, and what I found on my journey to my place in it. As an actor, I wanted to know what it would be like to act a part I found meaningful; as an activist–minded artist, I wanted to tell a story I was not hearing about the transgender experience I found myself living. I would have never expected that my personal gender journey would leave me, five years later, unable to tell my own story.

Imagine me in the year 2000: (I cringe at the comparison, but...) a little like Jenny on *The L Word*: observant, quiet, clearly lesbian but a nascent queer. I was Southern, too, which meant something about my naivety (but not, I assure you, about that of any other Southern queers). As a student of theater, I had been steeped in Shakespeare and Ibsen. Only after reading *O Solo Homo*, an anthology of queer solo performance, did I realize there was a whole iceberg of queer theater out there, while I stood on the mainstream theater boat, praying for a crash.

Like every other educationally over-privileged, upper- middle-class white kid, I found an internship that I hoped would deliver me to where I wanted to be. I landed a position as a research assistant to Holly Hughes and Alina Troyano (a.k.a. Carmelita Tropicana). As founding members, these raucous lesbian performance artists wanted to write a book to commemorate the twentieth anniversary of the WOW Cafe—a feminist (at the time, entirely lesbian and bisexual, but not, in my memory, trans) theater collective in New York City's East Village. I was to serve as their on-the-scene reporter, questioning previous and current members about the history and present of the space. The book never materialized, but my own aesthetic—and also my definition of my self—took root during that summer, bringing me to the still-evolving artist and trans man I am today.

I am not very adept at separating my personal experience from my artistic practice; indeed, the lines of my experience are blurred. As a college student, I connected to theater through the vital lifeline of the feminist, queer aesthetic I discovered at the WOW Cafe: the work put up a mirror to my life, when before, theater seemed like an oil painting, and dykes were never the subject. I also met the first person I ever knew to be a trans man during my stay in New York that summer. The very existence of him — him! — opened up my own story with new words, new possibilities for every body I encountered, but especially my own. What else is theater but bodies enacting words and possibility? My life became the subject of my art, both of which are shot through with a distinctly political aesthetic.

In New York in 2000, I saw Sarah Jones' *Surface Transit* at PS 122, a solo show on the complications of race and ethnicity that impacted my thinking for what would become my solo show, *Underground Transit*. I watched spoken word and drag king shows, and traveled to Rochester to watch Peggy Shaw look as good in a suit as I could ever dream for myself in *Menopausal Gentleman*. I rode the subway for days, seeing through sheltered eyes an unknown world of class, race, and gender, all sweating upon one another during the evening rush hour. I was a dyke with a trannie boy's life history, just learning the difference between sexuality and gender identity, on my first summer away from home, spending time at the WOW Cafe. I lived twelve blocks from Toys in Babeland. Holly Hughes and Carmelita Tropicana were my mentors. The drama wrote itself.

I returned home to Emory University in Atlanta to professors delighted by my new drive. They became important allies as I proceeded to find myself through my solo performance, reading drafts and giving notes at my rehearsals. It didn't matter that each of us was still learning how to define transgender identity. The lack of definition left me with only my own story to tell—that's the only appropriate mission after all. I read all of the feminist theater criticism I could find, as well as recent work in performance studies that assured me I could affect an audience as an activist, and how. I used my Women's Studies readings on gender performance to direct the way I embodied the shifting shapes of my gender identity with significant, performed costume changes on stage. I know well that identity can be wrapped up in a pair of Levi's or a dress: we assign boxes to people according to their presentation. I dramatized that trope in order to highlight it. I made it clear, through performance, that a body can—and will— box itself and burst out of that box again and again.

I began touring the show before I graduated from college, then continued to perform around the country at colleges and theater festivals. To this day, in 2006, the message and points in *Underground Transit* are unfamiliar, sometimes radical, to many audiences. I don't take any credit for that: it is our culture's imposed ignorance to and/or refusal of gender transgression and fluidity that make my personal observations interesting or important to anyone at all. Queers everywhere are making mind–blowing work far more

artistically and intellectually advanced than the story
of my own early journey, and they probably look
better on stage in their underwear than I do, too. The
impact of an artist's work depends on where ze meets
hir audience. I spend a lot of time with young people
very much like I was in the summer of 2000, and also
their parents, in places that are ideologically worlds
away from New York and San Francisco, where work
like mine abounds. For audiences that are already
allies to or participants in gender transgression, my
work is just another stitch in the tapestry.

I performed *Underground Transit* for two years until I
created my next show, *Debutante Balls*. Performance is
my activism, but my politics want more than to make
space for gender transgression. I live in the South,
honey, and that has made for more stories than I
could tell in just one solo show. I passed for a
privleges brought me, as a young adult, to not one,
but three debutante balls.

Some of you may be confused:
What's a Debutante Ball?
What's that got to do with being queer?

Well, for those of you who don't know,
and there are many!
Yankees, Midwesterners, and Southern born alike
The Debutante Ball is a rite of passage for the elite.

Young women and their families in the highest social
circles still refer to the process of entering society as a

marriageable woman of good manners as
Coming Out.

(Coming Out, in this context is like homecoming on
steroids,
prom on acid)

woman, and I passed for rich, too, and these
Depending on your city, your state, your
social circle,
you may come out at
sixteen, eighteen, or twenty–one years old.
You pray to get a summertime gala
or risk making your debut
in a long white dress
after Labor Day.

But isn't that what coming out is all about?
No matter who you are
when, where, why, or how you come out,
you are always just a girl
standing in a spotlight
awaiting acceptance in a long white dress
long after Labor Day.

You've gotta know how to make an entrance
how to be graceful, and take it in stride
if you want to survive.

—Excerpt from *Debutante Balls*

In *Debutante Balls*, I tell the story of coming out at three Southern galas, but never as a Debutante. I was always the friend of the Deb, and that peripheral perspective gives me all the room of a radical feminist queer nationalist peanut gallery from which to comment on the race, class, and gender issues inherent in such experiences (which, when overlooking a ballroom, can be quite large and nutty). In "real life," I came out first as a lesbian, then became an outspoken radical feminist, then (reference *Underground Transit*) turned inward to find desire and identity in myself, and then came out as trans.

That's a whole lot of transitioning
too much to describe all in one breath
but...

I think we're about ready for another
digression...yes?

Dance with me.

[*The sexy intro to a tango plays.*]

When you learn how to dance
I mean dance like a Debutante
you learn how to move
in a box made of a man's arms.
You learn exactly where to put your feet
on patterns already set out for you across the ballroom floor.

I learned to dance
on the feet of my fathers
tapping out the rhythms on the top of their shoes.

When I learned to dance
on the feet of my fathers
I didn't think of it as following:
I was learning how to lead.

I learned a different kind of dance
In the darkness of a dyke bar
grooving to a beat I liked better
but still didn't feel like quite my own.

Then I hit the ground
on my own two feet.

I started to dance my own
waltz–foxtrot–swing
and while the traffic of straight and gay
moved around me
around the floor
on different days
in different directions
I stepped out of the grooves
stepping on toes and bumping shoulders
as I made my own way.

Coming out trans felt like
catching the ground
learning to dance all on my own
learning that a dance *could* be my own

and that a dance works best
when two bodies
that know *themselves* move
and catch each other in the groove.

[*A chorus from Billy Idol's "Dancin' with Myself" plays
loud. Turner grabs people from the audience for a dance
party moment!*]

— Excerpt from *Debutante Balls*

Like most people, I struggle with labels. I feel I must
describe, if not claim, all the social factors that make
me who I am, a theme which shows up more didacti-
cally in *Debutante Balls*. I tick off the list of Important
Things I Learned in Women's Studies to enact the
message of the show: come out as you are, whatever
you are; to be specific, so that you see the many
places where you connect to the universal. When I
drag from my tuxedo into a ball gown, I intend to
make it clear that even when draped in all that you
were (your past gender presentation, your class, your
skin color — all of which become apparent on my
body with a single Jessica McClintock gown, who
knew?), the person standing there in the present
moment is always greater than the sum of hir parts.

But how do you market that? In four years, I have
struggled to identify myself not only to myself, but to
paying audiences as well. I was born Katie Kilborn. I
became, partly out of shorthand, but also because of
some misguided idea it was gender neutral, Kt

Kilborn. How I became Scott Turner Schofield is another, entirely personal story — but Turner, as I am known to most folks, seems metaphorically appropriate, no? For a while, I was a "lesbian skirting gender boundaries." Then I became a "trannie boy lesbian." Then a "dyke boy," and then, my favorite, "Whatever you want. Really." "Consider your audience" my marketing mind coos — but my "target audience" is anyone with a gender and/or anyone who has ever felt different. Easy, right? Except that we do not possess language to integrate ourselves meaningfully. To break it down into an unfortunate binary, which you should expand appropriately: how do you get a frat-boy — who may or may not be queer, but who is negotiating gender, acceptance, and community (differently, perhaps invisibly, but equally) as much as a trans person — to connect to the tag line for *Underground Transit*, which is: "A Spoken Word Queer Theory Rock Opera Passing as a Theater Show?" Without the tag line, how do you bring in the queers?

During my intern days, Peggy Shaw once turned to me in exasperation and said, "You really think there are answers, don't you?" I did. I do. And I am proved wrong over and over again.

I have named the curve of my belly, the one that stubbornly resists masculinity, my learning curve. You'll see it when I perform, before I take off my shirt to show you what's still there on my chest. My chest, my belly remind me and tell you — in case you didn't already know, because I forget all the time—well, I actually don't know what they remind me of, which answer I embody. Just that I do, and that it's complicated. Can we call that the moral to the story?

But it isn't over. In fact, I am finding a different story is just beginning. I began injecting testosterone in October 2005. The documentary *TransGeneration* and the movie *TransAmerica* simmered mainstream interest in transgender issues already heated by the antics of Rikki Wilchins, et al., and Hilary Swank's Oscar nod for *Boys Don't Cry*. My booking line started ringing more often, and my voice dropped about an octave in six weeks.

In late November, I performed at a state college in the Northeast. The show was packed beyond anyone's expectations, from the floor to standing, the room filled with the "perfect audience" I always seek: visible queers and sorority girls, jocks of every ilk, worried administrators, and eager professors. For the first time since my voice dropped, I asked the crowd, "Would you believe I was almost homecoming queen in high school?" A loud guffaw from a man in the third row, covered by a cough. Crickets from the rest. Eyes squinted, my audience checked me out from ass to chest to throat to crotch as I told them

> I don't expect you to see what's
> inside of me
> you couldn't anyway
> we're not trained that way—

to be sensitive.
I think it's a defensive convention
we're taught never ever to mention
anything a little queer
so of necessity
comes invention
The girls who feel like boys
start to dress in a way that says
yes
to anyone looking through
what we learned about style
and intention.

— Excerpt from *Underground Transit*

About two-thirds through, as I undressed to reveal
my bound breasts, a huge jock stalked across the performance space to the exit. He called me a faggot as
he went. I was singing *Boys Don't Cry* by this point,
so I called it synchronicity and used the energy he
raised in the room to round out the evening in
poignant fashion. During the post-show Q&A, someone finally asked the lingering question I felt, but
ccouldn't find: "So, you were born...what? A boy or a
girl? I can't tell." I realized suddenly that for some in
this audience, I had skipped woman entirely, I had
passed through man into trans woman — they thought
I was MtF. What does that do to my story? In performance, must I forever end emphatically a man for
my transness to make storytelling sense? Or did I
genderfuck myself out of my own fucking gender?
Can I continue to come out and be recognized as

transgender without having to tell a story to describe it? Or is storytelling, to myself and others, the condition of being—and staying—transgender?

I found an answer to that question in May of 2006, when a performance of *Underground Transit* was canceled by Central Piedmont Community College (CPCC) in Charlotte, North Carolina. This state-funded institution gave me an ultimatum: end the show fully clothed, or take your transgender body and show to another venue. The question became whether taking my shirt off and showing my transgender chest, unmodified by surgery but changed by hormones, constituted "nudity." I choose to disrobe in this moment as a final act of vulnerability before my audience. The effect in the audience, I have been told, is one of recognizing another human body—it is not shock value or titillation. This did not matter to the venue. A male actor playing Jesus in *Jesus Christ, Superstar* could perform at CPCC in only a loincloth, but, as the facilities manager said to the *Charlotte Observer*, "A man who has always been a man is different, I think. That's my own personal take on it."[1] If I have learned only one thing from my performance career, it is that gender is in the eye of the beholder.

The trannie boy taking T a few short months ago wanted nothing more than to pass, to live in my gender with a sense of privacy, to be able to choose when I tell the story of myself. Now that I do pass, I have found that I enjoy telling this story, that telling it on stage, and advocating for myself by going on T, has empowered me to tell it on the street. I find myself coming out to strangers, when I feel up to it, because that's the point of what I perform — why would I stop that activism just because you haven't bought a ticket? To some, this compulsion makes me less of a "real man." To some, I will never be a "real man" no matter how skilled my portrayal. Maybe, then, I will always be just an actor. If gender is performance, then y'all are my audience. Kindly turn your cell phones to vibrate mode.

HARD UP IN 2006
by Scott Turner Schofield
for the ever-inspiring Tim Miller

[*Turner walks on stage in chest binder and signature leopard print panties. Smiles at audience as they take in his trans body.*]

I was not born in the wrong body.
I'll show you.

[*Opens panties, says into them:*]

Get hard.

Come on!

Seeing is believing.
Be a man!

Prove to these people you're a man, man!

[*pause*]

Come on. Don't embarrass me here.

Get hard!

Get hard for the New Year!
Get hard to get the girls!
Get hard because you never know
which time
will be
the last time.

Get hard because it feels so good to be touched
even if you're only touching yourself.

[*Lights down. Rise again on Turner, hands in his panties.*]

Do we begin to masturbate to feel ourselves into
being?

Mine, the only touch I can feel, my own touch
on myself, my fantasies my own
locked inside my own head
locked in the bathroom
locked into the friction of me on myself.

I, me, telling myself through touch
that I was not born in the wrong body.

I masturbate a lot these days
I'm a teenage boy!
Again.
If testosterone's supposed to make you more
aggressive
then it's aggression asserted on
my
self
in the best way possible.

I was not born in the wrong body, even though I am
not sure whether I am the subject or object
of my own desire.
In these moments, I want to be
boy inside a girl, boy with boy inside
more than my own skin or will can provide.

Every day, three times a day
my mouth open with sounds I cannot speak
[*Turner reaches into the panties, brings out a lipstick,
draws a heart on the binder*]
I exist for myself.

[*With these lines, Turner strips the binder*]
When you open your body
you let yourself out.

[*With these lines, Turner strips the panties*]
So get hard.
Get hard because it feels so good to be touched.
Touch is all I have
in this absence of words to describe

this body, this fluid transition of me to myself
in a body that is not wrong.

[*Naked, trans, wet, and hard:*]

I will get hard
harder still
I resolve to genderfuck every day of 2006!
Even if,
no,
especially because
I am fucking
myself.

[*lights down*]

Notes

1. Julie York Coppin, "Former girl sheds shirt.
   Nudity?" *The Charlotte Observer* 11 May 2006
   <http://www.charlotte.com/mld/observer/news
   /local/14550344.htm>

Letterman

Jordy Jones

"LETTERMAN"

About Radicalia Feminista. Phallacies and Queeries: A Phaggot's Contemplations

Tim'm T. West

Radicalia Feminista proposes that men are themselves not liberated and therefore cannot liberate
women. I wholeheartedly agree. But I sometimes
wonder if we are even qualified to talk about men or
women except to make reference to phony and dis-
honest categories that we are made to believe are
imperative and truthful. It is my belief that it will not
be men who liberate women nor women who will liberate themselves, but a radically different species of
ex–men and ex–women who divest and agitate what
"male" and "female" have come to signify. What I am
interested in proposing is not some reunion of Yin
and Yang or the fusion of a male and female—happy
mediums that are grounded in refined lies. I'm not
interested in rummaging through history to find
some unsexed being who was free of a gender category. Just how liberating can it be for us to all imagine ourselves as mothers when mothering is so

enmeshed in an opposition to fatherhood? Perhaps we can all be sisters. For me, it is freer of significations than mother...which is a designation that is all too contaminated for my bittersweet tastes. Still, the sister becomes the wife and mother, so would we not be burdened with freeing the sister that is still a she? Is this why the some are eternally deconstructing his/story?

Radicalia Feminista doesn't seem to understand that there are those of us who "pass," not necessarily for the other gender, but for the men and women we are assumed to be. Will there be a struggle against what we represent — men who refuse the illusions of manhood and women who disidentify with femininity — when we cover a whole range of gender appearances (some of which appear conventional)? When amazons and the revolutionaries draw the swords to take off the male heads, will I lose mine? Will they have non-deliberately executed one of their warrior-allies? How can I protect myself if I am trapped in this male body, and my performance is not savvy enough to win favor with the mothers, and when the fathers are the ones I have to defend myself against? I'm concerned with finding ways to identify the men (and women) who are allies but who will be mistaken for enemies. Sometimes it gets confusing to try and figure out whether the warring you do is killing off the enemies, the allies, or yourself.

Radicalia Feminista proposes that men learn total autonomy and that we become "truly" rational beings. Indeed, male domination prefigures a code-pendent relationship. Men dominate others when they cannot control themselves. But what's up with these rites of passage she requires of men like me — the burden of proving that I am not a tyrant like the others. I am presumed guilty until proven innocent. And the trial? Desert/shun? I already know those sands. Tasted them when there was nothing else to eat. I recollect my thirst and hunger in equatorial temperatures as a personal testament of my survival. The desert's isolation can teach me autonomy and good sense no better than my own crowded ghetto streets.

I refuse to go into the desert to become a revolution-ary unless I can bring the monsoon with me; unless my solitude can call forth kisses of ancestors who did not fit a gender, but who were made to fit one. There have to be rites of passage that don't require discon-nection. I write and theorize in order to build a mon-ument for the dead that recasts them, not in the way some have come to know them, but as men and women restricted to half–selves in order to secure the patriarchal order. I want to erect a monument for ancestors who wept and screamed (sometimes in secret and at other moments violently) because of the burden between their legs and the tyranny that would define the rest of their lives because of it. It takes a brave soul to resist when resistance means death. That is why I forgive so many of the mothers and fathers before me — forgive them for their reluc-tant compliance to acting like a "real man" or a "real woman." I thank those whose silent resistance eventually consumed them. I thank the witches and warlocks who screamed anyway and who were burned for it. I thank them for bequeathing just enough of the anti-sexed and vulnerable spirit in them to me so that I would be more aware and better able to forge resistance.

Some of the feminists have written men wrong. What they write about men seems so non-representative of me. I have never accepted manhood, and most of my life have represented, only in form, that gender that is both defined by my biological constitution and a socially prescribed performance. Masculinity. Masks. I mastered them well enough to be marked as male. I am a double-crosser. Have always disturbed masculinity. I am a faggot/traitor to the male sex because I do not long to possess a woman. Many black women say that I am a waste and not a real man because I do not accept my rightful position as head of the black family. I refuse to donate sperm to replenish the earth with male (or female) revolutionaries who beat their wives. I want to raise anti-boys and anti-girls.

I held on for dear life to that vulnerability little boys are comfortable with until they are told that the feeling is reserved only for women and to maintain order. I am told that this emotionally exposed position is women's handicap. I infer that women's vulnerability is why men have believed that they are naturally qualified to rule over women. I do not wel-

come that lie, nor do I want any part in the
self–deception. I refuse to associate with men who
exploit women in order to make the lies seem worth
it.

Freud was such a punk. They idolize his prescrip-
tions. Dora should have owned a gun.

Men cloak the lack with violence. Each time he strikes
her body or spirit he is further removed from that
frightened boy within himself who fears that his
weakness will be uncovered. He reiterates the violence enough to himself and to women so that they
too will come to believe that the lack has been
erased — that his vulnerability has been undone. The
tyrant is nothing more than a punk who compul-
sively bluffs. Feminist Patricia Robinson was right.
The tyrant must convince his subjects that he is a god,
not vulnerable. But there is a problem. Each strike,
rather than erasing the vulnerability, comes to signify
it all the more. So some try to reduce the effects or
intensity of the blow with kinder and more gentle
acts of violence that do not scar the body. Economic
and social scars sometimes cut as deep, but we can
ignore the wounds, for they can be construed as
having origins that have nothing to do with sexist
violence: capitalism or women's oblivion to the small
strides given to them. I liked that about Feminist
Firestone. She calls Marx out on his blatant oversight.
Stabilize the classes, and there will still be a need for
battered women's shelters.

Vulnerability for some boys is such a terrifying bottomless pit that they strike relentlessly at everything, believing that even death and war and the battle scars are better than living with the "lack" that is open, fluid, innocent, peaceful...is genesis. That which some have come to regard as woman (the feminine) does not struggle against this "lack" to save her life. This is not the "feminine" script that men wrote for women to make them forget the vulnerability underneath their performances of mother, wife, daughter, whore. Some women have come to understand that they are being programmed to forget and hate the "lack" and are warring to get it back. This is a different kind of violence than the one men (and women frightened into docility) reiterate; for it is violence for and not against what is essential and true. Humans are essentially vulnerable—a lack and possibility that is never filled.

Then there are boys who are the anti–men men. Not those who do parodies on the feminine but who fix it all the more in doing so: the cross dressers who desire to be "real women." There are men who do a parody on manhood and who appear to be men. Exemplary mimicry. But is it mimicry if it is mistaken for something real? I presume that our satirical mastery of manhood is precisely why many of us have escaped being put to death. We terrify other boys because we infiltrate and mock masculinity. We are butch dykes with biological penises that we do not exalt. We refuse the primacy and supremacy given to the phallus but will use it to "screw" the man. Acting manly and having a cock makes it harder for the patriarchs to identify the traitor–men, and so we sometimes bark and pout and be afraid right alongside them just enough not to forget that they are wimps. We don't pity them. They have always had the option of being a different kind of man but like the benefits that come with patriarchy. They are my enemies even when they are the lovers of my sisters or brothers.

My pops might have become a male traitor. But he was weak and frail and afraid to bash his pops in the head for fear that he would get the beating reserved for his moms. He was weaker than the mother who beat him and locked him in closets without food. But he escaped and was taught the brutality that is the only option for broken ghettoboys. Hardness was and is still a pervasive untruth. It is spoken and spoken and spoken again in technosynthetic winds so much that many of us boy children no longer recognize its bitter sting in the throat or the way it makes our eyes tear. We are desensitized, crying without tears, and believing that we cry for no reason.

Uncle Sam say: "Punk." "Sissy." "Faggot." Pops wiped his tears away with knife blades and gun barrels. They did not absorb his pain. The tears just rolled off in Vietnam and on the southside of Chicago. He forgot his tenderness and became his father. And my father? Cycle. I someday want to hear his story of fear and self–loathing. I have tried to love him even when he has been abusive. Sometimes I am not sure how to love him when he is courageous enough to try and love me. I long to be a father...differently and similarly — recognizing the sweetness that came out of bitterness. It is all that I have.

Some of my allies are queer boys who are aware of the pitiful state of men — who know that women have been exploited because men are weaker beings and are not brave enough to live with weakness. Often women learn to cultivate this tenderness...except for the girls who scream because they should not be punished for being essentially human, essentially vulnerable. These are women who, like Audre Lorde, tell the truth about themselves even when death tries to steal them away. They are prophets.

Most girls grow tired of fighting the order of things as prescribed by capitalist, patriarchal society. Women too wear masks. My grandma, the Creek Indian, she did and was still driven mad. They say lots of Indian women are mad. As if there are not reasons why this might be the case.

I have learned that it is sometimes easier to wear masks and perform the designated roles; much harder to perform your way out of the script by inventing something new and not yet experienced. I have reiterated maleness just enough to get by. At times, I have felt trapped and have tried to find others like myself. Not those boys who, seeing the evil done to women after the lady doth too aggressively protest, decide to become more sensitive patriarchs. I have wanted to meet the boys who never "bought" the lie in the first place: that there was so much to gain from covering that lack, which is vulnerability, with our fists and howls and guns and bombs.

I cannot understand Radicalia Feminista and her voice. It screams an appropriated–half/woman–man trapped in defensive but anxious Western philosophy. Philosophy will have no part with what she is attempting to do, and so the words backfire and come out contorted. I have two philosophy degrees but refuse to write like that anymore. I don't believe that she really sounds like that. She makes no sense when she talks about sexual intercourse and even less sense when she talks about lesbians. Lesbianism can be incredibly political and subversive. Not the kind of lesbianism that Feminist Lila Karp talks about—the category created by Freud and his boys for their sexual kicks. Like the heterosexed, female homosexuality where women strike each other, and one is the breadwinner.

I experienced being a lesbian once. My girlfriend wouldn't let me use my penis, and it fucked with my head. I became more fully human and experienced a more fully eroticized body as a result. Marcuse and Deleuze said that this could happen. My girlfriend and I explored polymorphous perversities, and I was fine with being completely vulnerable with her. She even entered me once, and I wasn't afraid. But her girlfriends suspected that I was a fag–patriarch trying to convert an amazon...and eventually it got to her...and she left. But my being with her in that way was political...and not: it was because we violated the sodomy laws and not because her making love to me just was...nothing complicated. Not the result of feuding parents or teen rebellion, but an openness that is there in everyone but which I did not deny. Is that what lesbianism is? An openness and not a concealment? Many feminists don't understand. They have read too much Freud. They call him out for the lies he told, but he appears in their writing and analysis, laughing at his success. Feminist Lila Karp should have been more careful when she entertained his *Three Essays on the Theory of Sexuality*. It is fiction.

The ironic thing about reiterating the gendered performance is that one can begin to believe that the performance is real. Ironically, he or she must keep performing it so that the lie will not be exposed. Unfortunately, there are women and men who continue to do violence to the truth of the body each time they deny its vulnerability. But there is an agitated army of radical cloaking traitors just waiting to "come out" — a tribe of Judases who never bought that Jesus was king of kings. Just a genderless spirit: vulnerable and wanting.

Conformity and Transsexuality

Jay Sennett

LesbianHighFemmeFaggot
Gaylourdes

Say Hello

Gaylourdes is a queer genderfucker fascinated with
theories about bodies and music and ideas. Feelings.
Gaylourdes is intense and models himself on his gay
friends. He likes to speak in masculine terms because
it's easier being campy that way. You could call him a
drag king but the performance is not wholly unreal.
Surreal, more like. He's a pansy with a passion for
muscle marys: he has a weakness for kooky queer
types who love books about drugs and dancing and
performance. He loves a style of camp that is vivid in
visceral terms; he wishes there were more camp lesbians, so that he didn't have to rely so much on a
specifically gay camp aesthetic to be understood.
Then he wishes he didn't have to say lesbians,
because while that's the heart-shaped box that he

sprang from, he realises the ID tag isn't really what he's talking about. He wishes he could be in Manjam (a local male revue), he wants to perform and bring his masculinity to life, but he's not a self-identifying male, and people would probably think he's just performing anyway. He wants (dreams) to be lean and lizard-like, sinewy and wiry, 47 years old, smoking a rollie, and talking about dancers.

Reveal Costume

A performance, a tizz, a to-do. A squirming and uncomfortable spot, underneath the collar, getting hot and bothered. A scratchy wig itching, a sequined strap chafing, stockings rasping between legs. A binding that makes it hard to breathe. A hullabaloo. An issue. An awkward moment. A stare. A cowboy and a sailor, who kisses off my moustache, as they all watch and cringe. The mask has slipped, they crow. It's really a girl and a boy, they say. Snogging. And at a queer event, too. It was better when you were untouchable and your moustache in place. When you were a drag king, and we watched you on stage, and you made us laugh. When you performed your masculinity but we saw through it and checked out your lesbian tits. Oh it's a fine line. I love every bit of performing, of dressing up, the practice of rehearsing and refining. Of costumes that constrain and bind, that limit and extend, that confuse and revolt. I want my wardrobe to be all costume, all glitter, all tucked and tailored. Undressing, unpeeling, undoing, layers and layers, skins and skins. My friend said that we were all middle, not beginning or ending. All middle and brilliant intensity, fiery and full of sensations, greedy for experience. Sometimes it's far less about identity than a feeling of something that can flit between bodies, shudder and reverberate inside, that hot feeling in the back of your throat, a heady rush and hum in your ears as suddenly everything else is quiet, and you rest your heavy hand on the back of his neck, and press your foreheads together tight til the sweat runs down the side of your face.

Desire

Desire, privacy and disclosure, enclosure, including, deluding, delighting, confiding.... I'm on a swing in the park, swinging around these words, letting them ride up my chest like a singlet on a teenage boy in trouble. Sometimes I wonder if my genders are all metaphors, or additions, like souped up fenders on a flash Cadillac. Is this a case of wanting to have my cake and eat it, too? Recognising in the heat of the moment a boy's flushed face and exposed desire. There's all this cake around me; I'm swimming in it, swallowing in it, swallowing it in, consuming and turning myself inside out, cake with the jam and cream on the outside, pressing the icing together

inside and crumbs out everywhere, like broccoli flo-
rets. Crumbs to be sucked out between fingers, under
fingernails, sucked out and savoured, pressed against
the roof of my mouth. I have a writing project, and
I'm so excited! I hug myself again and again. I have to
make like an octopus and crawl across the floor
between aquariums. Step out in style, try to breathe
through my throat again, grounded and trusting in
these dreams.

I spent years working out what I should be, what
kind of lesbian I could be. Now all of that is suddenly
less important, I'm tired of looking at myself in the
mirror, searching for meaning in telltale signs of my
body. I want to forget about this body, let it recede
into implicit knowledge, like a skill well learnt, an old
automatic movement. We are moving light–years
ahead anyway, ten times the speed of fashion, like
Alice and the Red Queen flying across a chequer-
board landscape; we speed up til it's such a blur,
can't focus on anything, this rush, this speed, wind
whistling in your ears, the world spins past but really
it's us, transforming a thousand times over in each
moment.

Camp

I call myself Gaylourdes because I want to sound like
a gay lord; I want to convince you that I'm fey, gay,
camp, extravagant, easily swept away by grand

romantic notions. That I have an inclination to limp on my wrists and dream in queer times and places (thank you Halberstam, you old darling). I went on an enormous search once, for biographical data of the late fantastic playwright Sarah Kane, for just one source to credit her queer background, and everyone remained tight–lipped and silent, said she was just very private. Does it always have to be up to the queer press to claim our own? Being Gaylourdes is not just about being out, but being undeniably queer. You know, odd. A freak.

Camp is different from kitsch because it's genuine. A camp sensibility demonstrates an honest love of divas. The Lourdes appendage is a reference to Madonna's child—a hint of diva worship. I have to declare my diva heroes now, before I forget, before you never find out: Paul Capsis, Antony and the Johnsons, Nigel Kellaway, Tilda Swinton, Sex Intents, Glita Supernova, Chris Kraus, Farinelli. Angels of mercy. Freaks of the night.

Gaylourdes steps out as Fagulous. An easy–peasy, sleazy police detective. You gotta see him prance down the street to believe him. Late for an appear-ance in his platforms and tight flares, shaggy red mane streaming in the wind, Ray–Bans and teeth shining in the sun. Denim jacket with fake leopard trim. He'll casually drape his arm around anyone, curve his handlebar moustache into a proud smile, tip his leather cap to the ladies, kiss everyone's hands, slowly, reverently. He says he's thysexual. I believe he likes thighs. He's got a gig disrobing at Gurlesque — a bent dyke stripjoint. He's getting in touch with his feminine side.

You can tell I want to be a leather faggot, can't you? That I want a leather daddy for myself. Uh, if you wanna help me out....

Against Heteronormativity

Jay Sennett

I Can't Be Male
Nick Kiddle

"I can't be male – I want to have childen."

That was what I said to a trans woman I met online.
Trying to reach out to someone I dimly recognised as
a kindred spirit, I told her that I felt male despite my
female body; like many trans people I've met, she
assumed I was FtM. I felt compelled to explain that
my identity wasn't quite as clear–cut as my summary
had made it seem.

She responded that trans identities are rarely
clear–cut, that nothing was conclusive proof one way
or another, and that if I thought I was sort of male, I
probably was. As far as wanting children was concerned, she asked me to consider how many men
wanted to pass on their genes and ideals to the next
generation, and how many would love to give birth
to their children if biology allowed.

But it wasn't that having children would keep me from being male; it was that becoming male would keep me from having children. Transition, as I saw it, was a double-edged sword: as I embraced my male identity, I would be forced to let my female side die. And I wasn't sure I was ready to give up everything that made me a woman, especially since I would never be a bio man.

Testosterone could make me look, sound, and even feel more male, but it would never make me capable of fathering children. Taking it would effectively render me sterile, a genetic dead end, and I shrank away from taking that step. I wanted, if I could, to pass on genes as well as ideals to the children I was determined I would one day raise.

Hormones weren't the only thing I worried about. My partner and I had been together for six years and talked about how we would raise our children as if it were already decided that we would have some. When I imagined the children I would have, they had his eyes and hair: a combination of the two of us. But he identified very firmly as a straight man, and my exploration of gender questions made him uncomfortable. If I transitioned, even just socially, I feared it would be the end of our relationship.

My friends thought I was stupid to let that hold me back. "You have to be yourself," I heard again and again. "You can't force yourself to be what other people want you to be." But I couldn't see it that way.

The part of me that loved my partner and wanted more than anything to keep the relationship intact was at least as valid as this male identity that I still didn't know whether I was discovering or creating. Rather than choosing between my true self and what other people wanted, I saw it as a choice between what I knew I wanted and what I still wasn't entirely sure about.

I tried to compromise by living out my male identity in small, temporary ways. I bought a sports bra to bind my chest and a man's razor to shave the peach fuzz from my cheeks. I started using the name Nick, rather than my given name, Nicola. When I pitched my voice as low as I could manage, I was frequently addressed as "sir" on the telephone. It thrilled me: I wanted everyone to call me "sir."

My weekly or twice-weekly trip to watch my beloved Scunthorpe United in action became my testing ground for my passing ability. I would wear my binder—I was afraid to wear it all the time in case it irreversibly broke down my breast tissue—along with enough layers of men's clothes that I could look male in a bad light, and, for important matches, I would shave and apply aftershave. At soccer matches, I was secure enough in my identity as a fan among other fans that I dared try out things that would have scared me silly in other areas of my life.

This compromise gave me plenty of opportunities to learn how much I enjoyed looking, feeling, and being responded to as male, without having to put my female side at risk. But my hope that it would keep my relationship intact was in vain. With every piece of maleness I tried out, my partner and I grew further apart, until he declared the relationship over.

I had been proud of my ability to create meals from scratch; now I went weeks at a time without eating anything other than ready meals. I had written novels and dreamed of one day making a living from writing; I stopped writing and tried to find another dream. Defining my new self as nothing more than a rejection of what I had been meant that I could barely imagine a future for myself, but the only alternative I could see was pain.

I abandoned my attempt to define myself as either male or female. It had caused enough pain. And in any case, the question was irrelevant now. Whether I was male or female, I was the husk of what I could have been with my partner. What I had become wasn't worth the effort it would take to find the appropriate label.

I turned to a trans man who lived locally, who had helped me with passing tips, and who had listened to my back–and–forth agonising about whether I had enough evidence to consider myself trans. I asked him if he knew of any drugs that might ease the pain or protect me from future hurt. "Don't start messing with drugs," he said. "They don't really change who you are, and you've got enough problems without waking up one morning to realise you're an addict."

"What about testosterone?" I asked. "Is that a mood–altering drug? Can you keep yourself from getting hurt better now than you could back when you were running on estrogen?" If testosterone could do that to me, it would be the answer to all my prayers. I'd lost so much already that I would hardly notice the end of my female side. If testosterone was the difference between me and my partner, the reason he could walk away with scarcely a backward glance while I melted down with grief, if it could let me treat future relationships in the same way, I would grab it with both hands.

He thought about it. "I don't think I was all that different," he said. "I never got very involved in relationships, even as a woman."

"So if I transitioned, I would be just like I am now? A sensitive, emotional man that gets hurt easily?"

Yes, he said, but went on to say I shouldn't let that hold me back from transitioning. If I'd been certain about my male identity, I wouldn't have, but I only wanted something that would stop the pain, and it seemed that not even testosterone could give me that.

At first, my dream of a family went the way of all my dreams, but as the first desperate ache of loss faded, I started to look again at my broken dreams and work out which ones could be pieced back together. I still didn't want to love another adult and take the risk that my love would be rejected, but a child, who wouldn't care how I defined myself as long as I provided food and loving care, was a safer option. Rather than deny my capacity for love entirely, perhaps I could use that capacity as a parent.

I made no distinction between giving birth to a child and adopting, but I considered my chances of being approved as an adoptive parent and decided they were virtually nil. If I wanted a child, my only option was to produce one myself, and for the first time, I was actively grateful for the female body I'd always accepted as my lot. A bio man who found himself in my position — wanting a child but not a relationship — would need the cooperation of a bio woman for nine months. All I needed was the cooperation of a bio man for a few minutes.

But just as I hesitated over embracing my male identity, I hesitated over trying to get pregnant. Both were irrevocable steps, and I didn't want to rush into either without strong evidence that I was doing the right thing. And, just as there could never be any conclusive proof that I was trans, I could find no conclusive proof that pregnancy wouldn't do dreadful harm to either me or the child.

In the same timid way that I had approached my male identity, I tried to get pregnant by having one-night stands with men chosen for no better reason than their willingness to have one-night stands with me. They couldn't get rid of me fast enough afterwards, which just rubbed salt into the wounds of my partner's rejection. Because I lacked the courage to seek out sex at the right time of the month, I didn't even have the consolation of pregnancy. I was making things worse instead of better, and my life began to run away from me.

I gave up work because staying in bed, sleeping the days away was a more appealing prospect than being awake and facing the suspicion that things would never get any better whatever I did. When I had to be awake, I poured myself tumblers of Scotch to dull the pain or wandered the Internet in search of something that would distract me from my own gloomy thoughts.

Clicking on links from a friend's website, I reached an autism advocacy site that made me look at my struggle in a different light. Protesting against the attitude that autism is a beast that must be destroyed so that the autistic child can lead a "normal" life, the author pointed out that, "Autism is a function of someone having an autistic brain, and you cannot fight the autism separately, any more than you could fight the femaleness of a girl but not hurt the girl herself."

I'd considered the possibility that I might have Asperger Syndrome or high-functioning autism: that might explain why I couldn't manage my interactions with those around me and why I so often felt that there was a secret set of rules that I hadn't been told.

But my novel writing and my ache to be loved didn't fit the autistic profile at all. I couldn't explain them, and I wouldn't explain them away.

In the advocacy site, however, I found a metaphor for the way I was. I had often viewed my depression and difficulties with life as demons within, but now I wondered how much of the pain was just the natural result of living in a world that wasn't made for me. And when, elsewhere on the site, the author compared a wish to become neurotypical to a wish to die and be reborn, something resonated powerfully in me.

My friends, with the best of motives, had expected me to become such a different person that they, too, might as well be asking me to die and be reborn. They wanted me to respond to grief and loss the way they would because they believed it would make me happier, but they couldn't see how much it would change me.

My response to loss might cause me pain, but it had also given me the inspiration to create novels, novels those same friends admired. They thought I could suppress my grief without giving up my novel writing, and I didn't believe I was capable of splitting myself down that line.

Inside my mind, this realisation changed everything. But in my interactions with the world, it changed very little. Although I no longer believed my responses were wrong, I couldn't convince my friends of this, and they carried on trying to tell me how I should make everything better. And I still had to grieve: I might value myself, but that gave me no guarantee that the world would ever accept me.

Finally, life gave me an opportunity for pregnancy too good to turn down. A friend I sometimes watched soccer matches with, who had read and apparently understood my journal entries about my identity, decided he wanted to be more than just friends. I was afraid that a romantic entanglement would ruin our friendship, but when he offered to share overnight accommodations with me at a match, on a night I knew I would be fertile, the dream of having the child I longed for overruled all my other considerations.

I had vowed never to make myself vulnerable to a man again, but I broke that vow within a few days of sleeping with my friend. Whether it was my out-of-control hormones, which couldn't experience sexual arousal without making me think I was falling in love, or simple gratitude that he had given me what I most wanted in life, I started imagining we would forge a family together: him, me, and the child we had created together.

But even before the doctor could confirm my pregnancy, the relationship was floundering. He couldn't understand any of the things that mattered to me — he announced that he wouldn't be able to eat ninety percent of the foods I could cook and wondered why I saw that as such a problem—and he actively undermined my gender.

"I'm one hundred and ten percent heterosexual," he told me. "I'm a masculine man, and I need a feminine woman to complement me."

"If you were looking for a feminine woman, what were you doing with me?" I asked. "I'm not feminine. Not even close."

"Oh, but you are. I've seen you at soccer matches. You walk around at half-time to find your friends so you can have a chat. That's what a female brain does—it creates social networks. I've read books about the differences between male and female brains, and I have an extremely male brain."

I couldn't find an answer to that. How could I explain that I loved to be read as male and hated to be read as female to someone who thought walking around to talk to friends was proof positive that I had a female brain? We weren't even remotely talking the same language.

Female brain or not, he decided that sex with me would be inappropriate for his heterosexual self. Since I wasn't prepared to move halfway across the country to be with someone who couldn't allow me to define my own gender, he decided it was impossible for us to raise our child together and tried to steer me towards finding another man who could step into his shoes as a father figure. Another relationship had disintegrated into a painful mess, and this time I couldn't risk dulling the pain with Scotch.

I seemed to be making the same mistake again and again. Falling into relationships with men who couldn't accept my gender. For the sake of my unborn child, I knew I had to get help to understand why I did this and how I could stop.

I had seen a psychiatrist and a psychologist earlier in my questioning. I had wanted to know why I burst into tears at the first hint of frustration or rejection, but when I mentioned an argument with my partner over my gender questioning they decided this was the key issue. Because I wanted answers, I agreed to explore gender with them, but I spent more time trying to convince them of what I had already figured out than learning anything new.

At my initial assessment, the psychiatrist asked me whether I had sexual relationships with men or with women. My partner and I had often played with gender as a sexual role–play. I frequently took on the role of a man, occasionally with him playing the woman and more often with both of us as men. And even with straightforward sex, I could easily imagine that his cock was my cock, that his sexual responses were mine. While I sometimes imagined how I would be able to have sex with a woman if I were physically male, the idea of being with a woman as a woman held no appeal at all. I needed maleness to be aroused.

But in the clinical setting, I was too nervous to put any of this into words. The best I could do was, "With men, but in a sort of male way."

"You're not a pure transsexual," was his conclusion. "Although some people can be 'gay,' having sex with men really does mean you're taking the female role." He described me as having problems with my sexuality—whether because he thought that's where the problems lay or because he thought sexuality and gender identity were synonymous—and sent me to see a psychologist, who remained unable from start to finish to understand how I was defining my male identity.

Now, thanks to the mental health system, I had to go through the same psychiatrist to seek help again. I explained at length why I felt I needed his help, but he was more interested in discussing my gender. I told him that I had solved what I could and made a kind of peace with what I couldn't, but he couldn't see me as anything more than a case of gender dysphoria.

"I'm concerned about how you'll cope with becoming a mother," he said.

"Well, I don't think I will be a mother really. I'll be a parent, certainly, and the label for the parent that gives birth is the mother, but apart from that, I can't see much of a distinction."

"You won't just be a parent, though," he said. "You'll be a mother."

"No, I'll be a parent. Single parents all have to combine the mother and father roles to some degree—like my dad did when I was growing up. I don't see why it shouldn't be the same with me."

"Your father didn't want to become a woman, did he? Pregnancy is difficult for someone who wants to be a man."

I almost got up and walked out in disgust. How could he, who had no first-hand experience of either pregnancy or gender dysphoria, tell me what was difficult and what wasn't? I had enough problems to keep me awake as it was, without him declaring from on high that I ought to be worried about something that had barely even crossed my mind. But the only route I could see towards help with my real problems lay through him, so I made one more stab at explaining that I didn't want to be a man, that I wanted to live out my male identity in a way that made sense to me.

He asked if I intended to breastfeed. When I said I did, he sat back as if this proved his case. Pregnancy, motherhood, and breastfeeding, in his view, were so intrinsically female that they would fatally unbalance the psyche of anyone who considered himself to be male. Nothing I said could make him abandon this view, and nothing he said could make me accept it.

Even before I saw my male side for what it was, I thought of my capacity to bear children as a kind of consolation for all the things bio men could do that would be forever denied me. I could never have the male body I craved except in fantasy. Surgery could take me so far, at some risk, but no further. But my female body offered possibilities—pregnancy and breastfeeding among them—that bio men could never experience, and I was happy to embrace those possibilities.

When I first reached this conclusion, I didn't know how to explain it to the rest of the world. I thought that unless I could fit pregnancy and male identity into a theoretical framework that everyone could accept, I had to abandon one or the other.

Now, learning to value the self I've come to understand more than the self that others see, I can lay out what I believe myself to be and say, "Take it or leave it." I enjoy the things my female body can do—both sexually and reproductively—and I'm not going to pretend that I don't. I am proud of my long hair, even though I know I would be read as male much more often if I could bring myself to cut it short. And sometimes I act in ways that appear very stereotypically feminine. These are all part of my identity, too. I am not prepared to explain them away or bury them in the interests of establishing the proper "transsexual story." And now, I no longer feel I have to.

But the machinery of society—on which I have to rely for support—expects me to fit myself into the neat boxes of a form. In order to get proper antenatal care, I have to accept the label of "woman" from midwives and doctors, no matter how much of a lie it feels. And as my pregnancy progresses, the label comes more and more readily to everyone I meet. I don't enjoy it, but nor do I want to go into battle over it. I feel like a man, in the privacy of my head, and I'm learning to be content with that.

I still want to be read as male, and transitioning, at least socially, is something I plan in the future. I'm still afraid to let go of my female side, but that no longer matters quite so much. I don't have as much to lose now. My female body has done what I wanted from it.

FtM Blues

Jay Sennett

I hate when my dick falls on the floor...

www.jaysennett.com/blog

And Yet

Eli Clare

I lay out syringe, alcohol pad, vial: a ritual
connecting me to junkies. Draw the testosterone,
and push needle deep through skin into muscle.

    And yet, I would have chosen hermit, storm-high river,
    heron flying upstream.

Open the windows, forsythia spilling its dense yellow.

North on Baldwin Road, I walk my everyday walk.
Bottom of the hill, a dog barks, boy yells, "Hey mister.
Hey mister. Hey mister." We've traded names a dozen times.

Then "Hey retard. Retard. Retard."
School yard to street corner: words turn,
pebbles slung by the pocketful.

Crip skin marked,
white skin not.

Open the doors, daffodils rearing their bright heads.

Cypionate suspended in cottonseed oil,
a shapeshifter's drug the color of pale sunlight:

Voice cracks.
Stubble glints.

Open the cellar. Soon, soon the maples will be
unfurling their green fists.

    And yet, girl *arrived first, bones set to the current.*

In the mirror I wait,
the difference a simple ritual —
verb, skin, muscle, hormone.

Body begins.

Split the stone open, then the lilacs' deep purple.

At another time, another place, I might have relied upon
insistent dreams; gods, goddesses, spirits all;
an herbalist stepping out back, nettle or ginseng.

Jaw squares.
Hips and ass slim.

    And yet, had I been given a choice, they would have
    demanded clay or granite, salt water or fresh, as if the
    confluence could never be home.

Open, palms stretched wide, apple orchard still bare
boned, branch and trunk.

But today I have Pfizer, Upjohn, Watson,
doctors saying yes, saying no, judging
the very stretch of skin over bone.

Crip skin,
white skin:
which stories
do I tell
the best?

Body begins to settle.

Open to the peepers, coyotes, faint crescent moon.

This drug I shoot in careful fractions:
I step into its exam rooms,
pay its bills, increase its profits.

Pecs bulk.
Skin roughens.

Crip skin,
white skin:
which stories
rarely begin —
turn, flutter,
settle?

Let them draw my blood, check
liver, kidney, cholesterol, hemocrit,
track the numbers, write the script.

Open, the orchard soon to be enveloped in blossom.

Round the next bend, other boys want my name,
hand me theirs, ask as only 5 year olds can,
"Why don't you talk so good?" I shrug, keep moving.

Body begins to settle onto its foundation.

And yet, here at the confluence river and ocean collide —
current rushing head long, waves pushing back — stones
tumble one against another; logs drift and roll. Tell me:
where in this hiss and froth might I lay myself down?

T–Ball
Jordy Jones

Tool of the Patriarchy
Jay Sennett

I'll Show You Mine
Jordy Jones and Doran George

This piece is a version of an ongoing conversation between two cultural producers who are close, long–term friends. Each is seeking to expose to the other something of his own understanding of his complicated and evolving sense of himself as a gendered, sexual, thinking human being. There is no attempt to solidify a position or come to agreement since the underlying proposition is that, while individual integrity is of utmost importance, there is no singularly solid position to take and no right way to be a person.

Jordy Jones (J.J.) What is a man?

Doran George (D.G.) Help!

I suppose the easiest way to answer this would be to say he is a highly contested phenomenon. I'd like to say that what a man is depends entirely on self–identity. Anyone who says, "I am a man" is one. Defining sex by individual choice would be the most democratic solution and, intuitively, would be the use of the term that would result in the greatest happiness. It resonates with Donna Haraway's writing on the cyborg,[1] and the new political optimism the Internet explosion heralded when it seemed that virtual reality might hold the key to the collapse of essentialist identities. The first time I came into contact with any real "community," where this sense of possibility seemed to be manifest in people's bodies, was at "The First International Transgender Film and Video Festival" in London. I left carrying with me the heady sense of celebration of collapsing "sexed" identity into gender, the corporeal into the cultural, and, therefore, positing it as something that can be freely adopted.

But this proposition provoked some glaring tensions, particularly for some of the transsexual men. Along with the apparent "new freedom," I found myself carrying away questions that I couldn't quite verbalize, but they were shaped by a recognition that inside those tensions existed some important information. Not just for the evolution of transgender culture, but also for the way we understand the sexed body more generally. Considering this, my answer still seems to lie somewhere in the wake of those tensions.

J.J. Interesting, isn't it, how these abrasive undercurrents can become apparent and sometimes erupt into full-blown confrontation when a certain critical mass convenes. "The First FtM Conference of the Americas" in San Francisco, in August of 1995, drew over 400 trans guys from all over the U.S.A. and some from beyond its borders. There had never been that many FtMs together in one place at one time before. Since then, there has been at least one major conference somewhere each year and often several in different locations. It was in the days that Mike Hernandez has described as being "after the dinosaurs, but before the comet." Those were the years following initial community organizing but preceding the explosion of theories of (trans)genders in the academy and the popularization of the Internet that together helped fuel the current population explosion and genderfication of the FtM "spectrum."

At the conference, there was a lot of tension between the heterosexual men and the gay men. The gays understood that they were a minority and that the straight guys were the default mode, and the straight guys from the city were mainly accustomed to, and familiar with, gay trans men. But for many of the het men from more remote destinations, this was the first time that they had ever been exposed to even the idea of a gay trans man, much less with the reality of what must have seemed to them to be such an obscene concentration of almost unimaginable embodiments. Many of them were shocked, confused, offended, and threatened. A common comment was that gay FtMs "shouldn't exist." I was fortunate enough not to become privy to the ideas of how our elimination might be accomplished. Of course, they did not really want to "eliminate" anyone. But they did feel that we threatened their hard won maleness. To them, a (trans)man who slept with (bio)men was not "really" a man. Sound familiar? What happened in London?

D.G. It was 1997. Susan Stryker, Steven Whittle, Jay Prosser, and Chris Straayer attended. This was a post–comet atmosphere, albeit the early days. Some people wanted to expand their sex identity and sexuality through collapsing sex and gender in the configuration that we know it. They wanted to canonize otherness, claim this space as one where homelessness of the sexed body was celebrated. These people were some version of women who had been identified with some version of the lesbian spectrum, who were now taking testosterone and experimenting with their own sex/gender and the sex/gender configurations of those they were sleeping with. Others, transsexuals who were invested in being distinctly male or female, wanted to establish an authentic claim to conventional sexed identity. They were variously tolerant of or critical of the "gender fuckers," but it seemed to me that the collapse of sex and gender didn't meet the needs of their embodied trajectories.

I now wonder if those who were looking to debunk sex/gender categories wanted to create more space for their desire, whereas those who were attached to particular sex/gender categories wanted to create space for their own identity. I have understood from you very clearly that you are only sexually attracted to men who, when they were born, the doctor or midwife slapped them on the bottom and said, "It's a boy." How do you see the relation between desire and identity?

J.J. For me desire cannot be divorced from identity. But attraction is very different than consummation. Some attractions are best left at that. How do I know that all the men I am attracted to pass the baby-slap test? I don't. I can't. I may have been, and well may be, attracted to a transsexual man. In fact, I am sure I have been. But I don't actually go there. I have gone there, which is why I no longer do. Attraction is one thing. Then there is the question of whether the action that follows initial attraction is a good idea. There are all kinds of good reasons to leave attraction at simple attraction. I personally pass on far more attractions than I pursue. Most people have "deal killers," and I have my own. It's all good, but it's just not all me.

D.G. I wonder if there are any other things that you could clearly identify about your desire. What is the shape of your sexual attraction?

J.J. What a wonderful question. What is the shape of my sexual attraction? It is related to the shape of my desire as well as my identification: maybe they are second cousins. Its shape changes with its size. That is part of its charm.

It grows on its own or with a little help from its friends. But you are asking about men. I like all kinds of men. Dark is attractive. So are blue eyes. Slender and hard is lovely. So is muscular. Smooth is beautiful; so is clipped fur. I like guys who are sweet and smart and who have a solid understanding of their own personal power and life force. Brains are sexy. So is self–knowledge and spirit. I like men who take care of themselves and who have interesting lives and friends. I like complicated minds and simple hearts. Fearless eyes. Impeccable manners. Each individual man has small details that are nothing in and of themselves, but which acquire a poignant sharpness from their association with him. This one's mole, that one's scar, that single dense tuft of hair between his nipples, a streak of gold in a green eye, a regional accent: the heart–piercing specificities, his "puncta," to adopt a phrase from theories of photography.[2] These are the objects of desire. Praxis? Vanilla with sprinkles to triple–ripple kink: delicious.

D.G. I have had sexual relationships with both men and women and been both top and bottom. I have been with men who are only tops and men who are only bottoms. In these various sexual relationships, I have experienced my gender as shifting. The dynamic of a sexual interface is productive of my experience of my gender at that time. My experience of shifting identities depends on how I am positioned within a sexual configuration. This reminds me of Linda Williams' writing on porn.[3] One of the feminist writers who critiqued anti–porn feminism, she argued that when we look at porn, we can simultaneously identify within the picture. Indeed, when I watched some Internet porn where white girls were getting fucked by black men, I was turned on both by the thought of being the white girl and of fucking the white girl.

I'm currently in a monogamous, sexually versatile relationship with a man. The shift from "top" to "bottom" has sometimes been stressful. I think this has been connected to a strong attachment I've had to a male identity. This development in my gender pre-dated my current relationship, but within the relationship it was expressed as a fear that if I didn't censor behaviors that are "not male," I'd lose the relationship, and if he demonstrated behavior that is not male I would not want to stay with him. After watching the straight interracial porn, I have been able to allow myself to be a girl with a pussy and play with my sex partner like he's a girl with a pussy. This has expanded the range of my sexual behavior and the experience I have of myself during sex as well as given me confidence that our relationship is not based on either of us practicing identity in ways that limit us.

When I think about the possibility of having sexual relations with a transsexual man, I think about my friend Martijn from Rotterdam who decided to keep his pussy. He calls himself "a man with a cunt." I love the idea of fucking a man in his pussy but wondered what you think about this. Much of the transsexual identity politics seems to be about establishing oneself as unequivocally of the sex that one becomes. Does desire for a body as "sexually/physically ambiguous" in some way have a place in that politic?

J.J. I hope that you don't let anybody's politics stop you from fucking anybody else's pussy...if you and he both want it. Some strains of identity politics — transsexual and otherwise — are pretty repressive. They begin with an imperative to liberate and end up policing desire. "Membership" in a given identity category then depends upon subscription to a certain set of practices and can be revoked at any time. The categories congeal, and the prohibitions and dictates follow. Political lesbians in the seventies weren't supposed to penetrate one another's pussies. "Real" men don't take it up the ass. And gay men of course should *hate* pussy. Everybody knows that. But I know gay men who love pussy, and I know others who love to talk about their pussies. "J'appelle un chat un chat."[4] The drag queen popster Pussy Tourette never stops. Banging on the bars, she screams, "Free Pussy!" And in *Pussy's Boogie* she croons to the boy in the pickup truck, "Go faster, baby, don't be a wussy, then pull it over and PhuqueMyPussy!"[5] There are trans men who like to get fucked in their pussies and others who do not. There are those who like it, and who *do* use the word "pussy" and others who like it, but only if some other word is used. Taxonomies contribute to desire. What's that? "Front hole" is a popular euphemism. I personally find that term off-putting. Some guys say "cockpit," which is kind of cute and really ambiguous. It could mean any orifice that might hold a cock, right?

But this thing about checking the political wind to determine if some consensual desire is alright—that worries me. I am especially leery of those identity politicians who suggest that some desire, mutually held, is inappropriate for the willing participants. Men should not want their pussies fucked? Why not? What if that is what the pussies themselves want? Does that desire un–man the gay man, does it un–gay him, does it un–man the trans man, does it un–tran-sex or un–gay him? And who decides? Are pussy-boys girls? Chicks with dicks? Guys with pies? Are trans men *men*? Are gay men *men*? Of course they are…but then again, maybe they are not. It goes back to the riddle of definition again. Speaking of defini-tions, how—and as what—do you see yourself now, and how has that changed over time?

D.G. I've been going through an identity crisis for the past twelve years. As I said, in the last three to four years I have strongly identified with masculinity, but when I was attending "The First International Transgender Film and Video Festival," I was some-times passing as female and sometimes sporting a genderqueer look. I described myself as neither male nor female. So I've been swinging backwards and for-wards, very slowly, over three or four years at a time between some version of male and some version of female. As my confidence in my relationship with my life partner has grown to express the range of possibilities that I am, I have developed a really clear picture that, quite apart from sexual play, in the rest of my life, there are times when I feel female and times that I feel male. I mean the way I feel myself emotionally in relation to other people or circumstances I find myself in, particularly. The words feminine and masculine seem a little reductive as ways of explaining this, but they certainly stem from those archetypes. Is your experience of your own gender multiply faceted, and if so, can you describe how?

J.J. I am not an overly masculine man. I'm not an utter flamer, but I don't think I am a particularly butch man either. I was never a butch woman. Was I ever a woman? I wonder. People used to ask "What are you?" and my answer – for years – was, "I am a freak of nature." It was intended to be funny, but it was also dead serious; it was the only explanation I could find. I don't think of myself as "straight acting." Are musical tastes gendered? I like torch songs and lounge, soul, R&B, jazz, and electronica. Verve remixes are thoroughly transgendered: two turntables, Cole and Ella. Who could imagine? Bowie saved my life as a kid. He was the first thing I saw in popular culture that seemed to really mirror my psychic life. I liked his shameless ambiguity and constant self-recreation and the possibilities that shifting represented. My own ambiguity was tinged with shame, and my sartorial recreation provided me with a self-protective satin shell. In my elegant glam stage, I inhabited my skin like a strange sea creature camouflaging itself with bits of detritus from the attic of the modern. I wore billowing Victorian men's shirts and velvet jackets over tight black jeans and elf boots. I wore things into the ground that should have been in museums.

You ask about my experience of my own gender, and I talk about music and clothing. I think that you want something more internal, and I am not trying to avoid that. Rather the inside points out—and vice versa. The inside experience and outside expression interrelate and are visible to one another. My psychic condition—including my gender—is certainly multi-faceted (the best gems are) and resists easy categorization. That is why I keep bringing it back to the concrete. Songs and shirts are rich metaphors. All our lists are. They defy the logic of either/or by bringing into our understanding entire worlds of tastes, preferences, and proclivities that provide us with points of tangency and divergence that show us the ways in which we are both like and unlike others.

D.G. It's interesting that you would talk about how we find out who we are in relation to others because the man and woman that I feel myself to be at different times are a picture I have of my mother and father; an embodied picture. This gendered matrix is built around a framework of trauma. The woman inside, me as my mother, believes that all men will abandon her and that they are inadequate and cannot give her what she needs. When she achieves things on her own merit, she is doing it not because it is exciting and empowering but because of her bad luck with men. The man inside, me as my father, feels like he can't manage his own emotions, particularly his temper. He feels that he is too aggressive for any woman and that when he is with a woman, she is always on the verge of leaving him. His self–image hinders his effectiveness in the world, making him feel inadequate and lowering his self–esteem.

My parents were actually both very practical. They created a beautiful garden, and we ate most of the fruits and vegetables in our diet from it. My Dad built our beds, encouraged us to see many possibilities for ourselves, took us to amazing remote places, and did a good job of providing for us. My Mum made all the preserves we ate, most of the bread, she even made our clothes when we were little. She gave me a strong anti–racist conscience in a very racist environment, championed all my endeavors to be an artist, and contributed to our family income. But from the age of sixteen onwards, my parents' marriage slowly deteriorated until, when I was twenty-six, my Mum left my Dad. I don't know why they split up. The difficulty they both had with masculinity is very understandable when I consider their family histories, cultures, and personal circumstances. But whatever their reasons were, I clearly learned their limitations and live those limitations sometimes. When I do, I experience myself as this embodied picture that I have of them. This seems to be the time that I feel most "gendered."

Sitting here now with you, I can feel my genitals between my legs, my eyes looking out at the world, my clothes against my skin, and the flesh beneath it. I feel myself, but I don't feel like I am a gender. I'm struck that gender is something that I identify as being exterior to what I feel is my "real" self. When I am the woman or the man that I mentioned, it's definitely me doing the actions, saying the words, and feeling the feelings. But alongside all of that, the gender neutral me that is sitting here with you now watches that man and that woman, almost aghast.

When I travel, cook, grow plants, or exercise any of the good things I learned from my parents, I don't feel gendered. I remember them fondly and relish my legacy. But I don't feel like I'm embodying them. I feel like me. The time I feel gendered is when I am experiencing limitation. So I have great fear of both the woman and the man inside me. For some reason I have identified myself with the behavior I learned from my father and my mother that caused them to separate and eventually divorce.

In my teenage years, I responded by rejecting traditional masculinity, under the influence of eighties feminism. These days I've become interested in it again. I've wanted to throw out all the self-evident critiques of masculinity and reinvestigate it as a culture that might have some useful information for human evolution. Are there any things about masculinity that you feel similarly about?

J.J. What is traditional masculinity? Do you mean the traditional masculine virtues? Strength, courage, protectiveness, honor, trustworthiness, respect, emotional reserve? I doubt that's the traditional masculinity that you rejected. What feminism were you influenced by? Dworkin or Irigary? Raymond or Stone? Very different. There is no single feminism. The strain that countered the image of the weak, hysterical woman with that of the brutal, violent man was just trading in stereotypes. More of the same; less of the different. Real men aren't caricatures any more than are real women. There is no "Great Oppressor." There are instances, specificities, alliances, ruptures, convergences, divergences, tangencies, and people, men, women, neither, both…of all sorts. A great proliferation. Masculinities are also multiple, and seldom, if ever, discrete. Purity is a great myth, a very dangerous myth. Chemicals, hormones for instance, do matter, and that is something that it is still not quite "alright" to talk about. Whatever the political bent, there is this sense that some things cannot be said. That is not only true of the socially conservative politics in which God and Family are diametrically opposed to Science and the Homosexual. "Progressive" politics has its own repressions. Chemicals matter? Yes, they do. This is not an anti–feminist statement. Equality need not insist upon equivalence. And difference should not be used to justify discrimination.

D.G. The masculinity I was rejecting is definitely the picture I had of low self–esteem, temper tantrums, feelings of inadequacy, inability to give a woman/other life partner what they wanted. The feminism was whatever I heard coming out of the small town women's group in the British, working class, rural–midlands, market and hosiery town where I grew up—the Hinkley women's group. Four of my closest school friends were attending along with six or seven other women. I wanted to attend, because my friends did, and because an investigation of human behavior was underway that I had never heard of before. I hoped they would have some answers to the questions that my struggle with gender posed. Some of their platitudes about being male were very negative, but I hoped that somewhere in this ideology was an answer that the masculinity I was running from in myself, in my father, and in the men I was attracted to, was something other than the chemical kind. I'm insecure about my masculinity. What is it that gives you such confidence about your status as male, and do you have any insecurity about your masculinity?

J.J. How nice of you to attribute such confidence to me. I'm not sure that it is entirely deserved, but I act "as if" and that draws responses that tend to rein-force that positive position. It is more a type of prac-tice—in the dharmic sense—than an essence. Which is not to say that there is not something akin to an essence; I suspect there is. I don't see that "essence" as existing separately from social construction though; I see them as mutually reinforcing one another. My childhood playmates accepted me as a variety of boy, and that reinforced the characteristics that I was exhibiting that led them to that interpretation of me. I am conscious of my difference. I work with what I have and choose to emphasize my blessings rather than dwell on my deficiencies. Insecurity works through fear of loss. I have faced and survived the greatest threat to masculinity, transcended the regulatory fear of castration. It has no power over me. I am free.

D.G. My only real source of confidence that my identity is male, is my body, and even that gives me trouble sometimes. When I was a teenager I was convinced my hips were growing and soon my whole body would be that of a woman.

J.J. As a very small child, I thought that I had a medical condition that my parents had inexplicably forgotten to tell me about. I fantasized about an upcoming birthday. They would say, "Now that you are five, it will begin to grow." I knew about "it." Mine was wildly undersized compared to those of my male playmates, but it was perfectly visible. There was something there; it didn't look like the slits of the little girls that I knew. The boys I played with explained me away with, "Jordy's balls are inside." Our early childhood experiences are so important in setting the tone of our lives later. What were you like as a child?

D.G. The childhood experiences that set the tone for my current questions about masculinity are the chemical ones. Those connected with violence. Bullying was very common in the culture I grew up in. I hated it, but I also loved it. My older brother beat me up throughout my childhood. I hated him for it, but sometimes he would also sit on top of me and tickle me to the point that I almost pissed myself. I would scream "I need to go to the loo" again and again; my words would get faster and faster melding into each other "nigoloo, nigoloo, nigoloo, nigoloo." We would both laugh about this made up word, a private joke between us. But very often I would run to my Mum, my Dad, my Aunty for respite. Sometimes I got seriously hurt. I remember once watching my Dad beat my brother up in front of company because he had hit me, and I was crying. Seeing my Dad's large body lose control and hurt my brother scared me.

At school, I hated to witness people bullying other people, however much I liked or disliked the victim. It made me feel dead inside, depressed, helpless, because I didn't know how to intervene. Usually, I was too invested in being one of the bullies, being in their "gang." There were kids at school who didn't appear to be involved in this cycle of violence, but I didn't want to hang out with them. I had a best friend at school for two or three years who bullied me constantly. I don't know why I didn't just get up and walk away, sit with someone else. I guess I thought he'd follow me, and if I'm honest when I think of him now, I hated him, but I also found him irresistible. He was dynamic, loud, exciting.

This highly suggestible, incredibly sensitive, scared, extroverted child that I was also had his own flip outs. I bullied other kids from time to time. From then until now, I have experienced moments when my body takes over. It's like a shock sears through my body; I lose control and break things sometimes, say mean things, storm out. I've even hurt myself out of frustration. I know women who were bullies at school. I was bullied by girls in my early childhood. I know women who lose control the way I do. My mum had a temper. But this issue for me is the man inside me, that's my picture whether or not it's correct. It's me as my father. So when I talked earlier about reinvestigating masculinity, what I was referring to was this, the place where I lose control.

It seems ironic that despite all of this, I know that sometimes I am afraid of engaging in behavior that seems too feminine. But I can also find it upsetting when people assume that I will behave in a certain way because I am male. Male and female feel like "traps." Do you feel any gender traps, behavior or identities that feel taboo for you, and you can't really explain why?

J.J. Well, I try to avoid foreclosing certain behaviors or avenues of expression based on stereotypical expectations of gendered behavior. But yes, I know what you mean. I suspect that I experience it differently than you do. Or maybe not. I wouldn't want people to think that I was not really a man. But isn't that how people police one another's gender? "Men don't...." "Only women...." Maybe for me it is a bit more literalized, because people sometimes look for clues, proofs of origin, evidence for an essentialist project. If I refuse to classify or to name myself, others will name me. I may not like the names. My name for myself may be incomplete, but in the naming itself, I claim agency, and in an optimistic project, that claim is crucial.

D.G. What is useful about having the terms male and female for human beings?

J.J. There is this idea that is popular right now, the idea that labels are somehow bad in themselves. Labels are something to hate without needing to think. Continuing the label metaphor, if there are no labels, we have no clue as to contents. But a label is no guarantee of accuracy, and this is where the "Down With Labels!" crowd has a good point. Outright mislabeling can occur. Or, labels can be incomplete or partially inaccurate. Then there are those overly tenacious labels that leave ugly grey squares of adhesive when they are removed: traces of the mislabeling that alert everyone that a change has occurred. Is this a reason to do away with labels entirely? We use language, including words, gestures, signs of all kinds, including "labels" to make ourselves (even marginally) understood. But there is always a gap in that understanding. The words we use always fall short...but without them we risk unintelligibility.

Sometimes I think we get so caught up in our little worlds that we forget how small they—and we—really are. I see this a lot in the academy and especially in queer studies. There is this naïve (in my opinion) idea that if somehow we can just dissolve the "sex/gender system"[6] we will be free.

D.G. The naïveté that you are referring to is brought into sharp focus for me by an e-mail I recently received. It was a request to sign an Irish trans woman's petition to be imprisoned in a women's jail rather than a men's. Her struggle makes clear that identities accrue meaning through material, legal, and historical conditions. Her safety is at stake regardless of the arguments. Interestingly, however, a gay man's safety would also be at stake, although his identity is not an issue. The danger for both is that of being trapped in a culture that will police with violence bodies that don't fit into either traditional masculine or feminine categories but which straddle them in some way. To be effective, we ought to be arguing for a penal policy that takes things on a case–by–case basis. This avoids the problem of putting the definition of woman back in the hands of the law.

J.J. But even if it were possible to do away with the sex/gender system, most people do not want a world in which gender neutrality is the new norm. And these are not just the bourgeoisie "heteronormative" Christian white male Americans who have assumed the position of bad guy in this new secular dogma. Most transsexuals, homosexuals, heterosexuals, bisexuals, ambisexuals, and bambisexuals are invested in gender as a category of human social intelligibility. Should their investment be overturned in favor of a theory of genderless utopia? This is not to suggest that the rights of the genderless or genderfluid or genderqueer should be ignored or diminished either. "Gender" itself is not the problem, though. It is used as a tool for control, and that is a problem. Excluding people who belong in a particular community from that community is a problem. And annexing someone into a community they do not belong in is every bit as obnoxious as excluding those who do.

D.G. In the performance you did last month,[7] you talked about a cross–dressing butch dyke grabbing you on the ass at a Frameline[8] event and saying that she wanted to have "fag sex" with you. I can see that she was freeing up sex and gender for herself, but by roping you into it, she was ignoring your boundaries and erasing the difference between you. I wonder if you could define the difference between sexual harassment and flirtation.

J.J. There's an expression, "Your right to swing your arms around in public ends at my nose." Random ass–grabbing is boorish. I don't know if I'd call what she did harassment. I didn't use that term. I think of "harassment" as mainly a legal term involving employment situations, although, of course, I under-stand that it extends beyond the legalistic definition. I did say it was not okay. It was not. It was crude, not to mention ineffective. My opinion of her plummeted.

Flirtation, when done well, is a subtle and interactive art. It starts slow and accelerates, fuelled by positive feedback. The initial approach should be ambiguous. No one should be uncomfortable, and no one should lose face. First touch should be on the arm or shoulder...not the ass. That is...if the point of the flirtation is to gauge sexual interest. Sometimes flirting is fun just for its own sake, but that can be a tricky game!

D.G. What are your favorite things about being a gay transsexual man?

J.J. Well, I think it has given me some unusual insight. I don't mean that in the obvious way: the cliché people (usually non–trans people) use about seeing life from "both sides." That is not something that I have personally experienced. But rather, growing up as a categorically difficult creature for people to place, I learned to notice categories and the repercussions that sometimes ill–fitting placements had on those placed onto them. I was different, and I learned to see others' differences. I was also similar and learned to see others' similarities. So...what are your favorite things about being...whatever you are?

Notes

1. Donna Haraway, *Simians, Cyborgs and Women: The Reinvention of Nature* (London and New York: Routledge, 1991).

2. Roland Barthes, *Camera Lucida: Reflections on Photography* (New York: Hill and Wang, 1981).

3. Linda Williams, *Hard Core: Power, Pleasure, and the "Frenzy of the Visible"* (Berkeley: University of California Press, 1999).

4. Sigmund Freud, "Fragment of an Analysis of a Case of Hysteria ('Dora')" *The Freud Reader*, ed. Peter Gay (New York: W.W. Norton, 1989) 196.

5. Pussy Tourette, *Pussy Tourette in Hi-Fi!*, Feather Boa Music, 1993.

6. Gayle Rubin, "Thinking Sex: Notes for a Radical Theory of the Politics of Sexuality'" *The Lesbian and Gay Studies Reader*, eds., Henry Abelove, Michele Barale and David Halperin (New York: Routledge, 1993).

7. Transforming Community at the San Francisco Public Library, Oct. 29th, 2005. Curated by Michelle Tea.

8. San Francisco International LGBT Film Festival.

FtM on a LGBT Panel
Jay Sennett

"Trans"? "Butch"? "Man"?: On the Political Necessities of Trans In-coherence

Bobby Noble

To a certain degree, this essay will seem a little like the body in which I'm currently living: a little mixed up; sutured together (with seams showing) from parts of my working class lesbian past; my history as a white butch and now, white man; a whole lot of my desire as an able-bodied, queer-identified, heterosexual boi who proudly claims a space as a mannish-lesbian; and a trans feminist, anti-racist political and academic practitioner (I am a women's/gender studies professor); all at exactly the same time. The essay, like my life, body, and sexuality, calls for a practice of what I'm calling in-coherence for trans men, white trans men in particular. These spaces of identity in which we live — whether they be boi, lesbian, butch, trans man, invert, and so forth — are historically shaped (what is practiced now may not have been thinkable thirty years ago), intersectional (informed by many discourses such as race, class, ability, nation, ethnicity, age, sexual orientation), but neither are any one of these reducible to the other in terms of definition (to be a trans man of colour means facing very different issues than a white trans man, even inside of our home communities).

In order to move beyond lip service to difference amongst us, I suggest we instead seek out in–coherence, which is the productive failure to cohere as a self, as a gender, as a race, as a community. This sense of failure need not be dangerous. It can be one very important way of challenging assumptions that somehow "we" have enough in common to form a "we" to begin with. Before "we" can be posited, we must first seek after an elaboration of the ways that "we" as trans peoples are not only different from each other but, to echo Audre Lorde, are the very site of difference itself.[1] Lorde's imperative reminds us, especially white trans men, that instead of assuming that our political work is over once we arrive in our chosen genders, we rethink our relation to power. We must, instead, posit that our political work, as whatever kind of men we may find ourselves becoming, is only just beginning.

Morphing Selves

Let me describe what I look like now. I'm white. I have beard stubble on my masculine face. My hairline is receding. I'm flat chested, with smallish (ok, smaller) hips, spouting what I call my man–belly, and possessing a deep gravelly voice.

Four years ago, if you had seen me in a bar before my supposed "transition," you would have called me a big butch daddy dyke. I was one of the big time dyke activists. Like many other dykes around me, I never would have considered becoming a man. It just wasn't, or so I thought then, on the political horizon. The choices that I faced circa 1978 did not include the possibility of changing my body to suit what would emerge as my gender.

At that time, I had found, for awhile, a reasonably comfortable home in the word "lesbian." This is a history I claim without ambivalence. I had come out as a white working class dyke in my last year of high school, 1978. I had found the word lesbian in the very important book *Lesbian Woman* by Del Martin and Phyllis Lyon, and after asking myself, "Am I that name?," I had answered unambiguously, "Yes." Part of what had appealed to me then were the political imperatives of being lesbian. Looking back now, the space of lesbian seemed like one of the few that had existed for queerly gendered folks like myself.

After a brief stay in late 1980s Toronto, I had made my way west to Edmonton, Alberta where I spent almost a decade working inside the lesbian feminist movement. My preacademic résumé details much of this work: almost four years with the Edmonton Rape

Crisis Centre, a member of the lesbian caucus of the Alberta Status of Women Action Committee, organizer and participant in many Take Back the Night Marches. I was one of a very small group of people to organize and march in Edmonton's very early Gay Pride Parade (circa 1987). I've spray–painted the sides of more buildings than I can remember. My feminist poster archive includes not only an original 1979 Toronto IWD (International Women's Day) poster but also a huge, very battered YES poster, which was part of the 1976 American ERA (Equal Rights Amendment) campaign. I started and sustained through two Edmonton winters a sex worker advocacy group called the Alliance for the Safety of Prostitutes, a group that met, during the coldest winter nights, in the only gay bar in Edmonton.

I was "the" out dyke for many television and radio interviews and published many activist articles, pamphlets, and tracts in a variety of feminist and lesbian feminist newspapers and magazines. I've helped build many parts of our activist movement and did so as an out and proud butch dyke.

I don't find my home in the word lesbian or dyke any more. The spaces marked by each of these words, spaces in which this same male body lived, are part of my being, part of my flesh. They are not just past tense but current in the way in which I live my life now, as a heterosexual guy who, unlike my former daddy–dyke self, is far more boy than man. Is it really so easy to wipe away what 30 years of living in dyke circles has taught me? There are few ways to mark this space of contradiction. So I cultivate paradox as the only way to keep these realities as simultaneous.

In language I might call myself a guy who is half lesbian. What does it do to the shapes of our gender and sexual categories when I can call myself "a guy who's half lesbian" and have it be true? Would that expression even have been possible a century ago? What makes it possible now?

Shared Histories?

Women living any kind of lesbian or masculine life at the beginning of the 20th century — those labeled with the then popular term "inverts" — would have understood something about the anxiety producing these questions even if their precise terminology wouldn't have been familiar. For instance, for Stephen Gordon, the main character in the very early and popular lesbian novel The *Well of Loneliness* by Radclyffe Hall, feeling like and being named after a boy was certainly what made her different, even if "feeling like a boy" was as close as, well, he, could get to becoming a man, at that historical moment prior to the emergence of gender transition technologies.[2]

In many ways, Stephen became the prototype of early 20th century lesbian life as prefigured by late 19th century sexology. The term invert marked those "women" who understood themselves to be very masculine and who might have made the choice to transition had that choice have been readily available. Sex reassignment modalities—breast reduction surgeries or breast removal with male chest surgical reconfiguration and weekly testosterone injections—were not readily available in Radclyffe Hall's time.

If they had been, I'm convinced that Hall might have told a story very similar to the one published in Leslie Feinberg's 1993 *Stone Butch Blues*, over 70 years later, even as Feinberg's text articulates a very different racial consciousness than Hall's. The main character of Feinberg's novel set in the American 1960s, Jess Goldberg, accesses surgeries, finds hormones, and entertains the possibility of a life lived half as a butch, half as a guy, and a bit of something else in the end. Jess, like me, may well have answered yes to that question, "Am I that name, lesbian?" Jess may well have answered no at the same time. Trans, inverts, and butches certainly seem to share a common history. Transitioning between these spaces is certainly made possible by scientific and medical advancements and by trans friendly physicians and surgeons who are advocates, not the enemies, of trans peoples. Like many others, I would have lived out the rest of my life as a butch dyke had it not been for Feinberg's book. Then again, if I had been born at the beginning of the century, I may have lived out my life as an invert.

One of the steps between "lesbian" and "trans guy" in my own history (and this is not always true for every trans man or FtM) has been living as a masculine lesbian, too. In her essay, "Man–Royals And Sodomites: Some Thoughts On The Invisibility Of Afro–Caribbean Lesbians," Caribbean–Canadian writer Makeda Silvera details the way that some dykes have always lived in "mannish" spaces.[3] Gayle Rubin argues something similar in her essay called "Of Catamites and Kings: Reflections on Butch, Gender, and Boundaries," where she also writes about these spaces of female masculinity.[4] These and other writers explored this queer gender long before the important work by Judith Halberstam named these spaces those of female masculinity.[5] There have always been butches; there have always been mannish women; there have always been embodiments of female masculinity.

But let's face it, as much as there might be a shared history, being a butch is not the same as being a trans guy, which is not the same thing as being a guy, even though I certainly can claim all three at exactly the same moment. I'd be lying, though, if I also didn't acknowledge that my daily life now as a guy is different from my daily life as a trans guy, different again from my daily life as a butch. Despite the fact that butch and trans might share a family resemblance with the early invert, they are each still separated from each other by history and what historical changes make possible. Trans, despite the fact that it's become a flavour of the month, is still a heavily regulated medical identity.

Like many other trans folks, I spend at least one hour a week in medical clinics waiting for a testosterone injection. To each doctor I see, I continue to produce explanations of myself, especially since I've not changed my official gender identity from F to M. Trans youth are in even more precarious situations than I. As the Canadian Broadcasting Corporation's (CBC) *Fifth Estate* program demonstrated recently in their documentary on young FtMs, trans youth are doubly, and sometimes triply, managed by legal guardians, physicians, and the scrutiny of "curious" onlookers, who just don't see the difference between trans and butch.

Testosterone compels me into those clinics each and every week. Testosterone changes my body, building up muscle, shifting fat from hips to belly, changing not just my hairline but also my facial structure. Now when I look into the mirror, I see someone—a gendered self I recognize—even though that someone looks a little like a brother to my former butch self. I still see her, too, in my face, but it was that gendered self that I was trying to effect with clothes, a Zippo, a brushcut, an attitude. But for many, like me, who transition, the attitude just wasn't enough. I needed masculinity as a second skin, not as something I wore over that skin.

Butches still face hostility and violence in their lives every single day, an experience passing trans guys may not share in the same way. To be a masculine woman, mannish even, is still to live a scorned identity. My daily life includes a much smaller portion of hostility, even if I still have to produce an explanation for myself, and a much larger portion, when it's there, of acceptability as a (male) human being.

Racialized In-coherence

That acceptability is not without its price. In *Stone Butch Blues*, one of Jess's best friends, Ed, commits suicide and bequeaths to Jess a very important book. That book was W. E. B. DuBois's *The Souls of Black Folks*, which forces Jess to think about the differences — rather than the similarities — between them. Ed leaves Jess a final message underlined in DuBois's book:

> It is a peculiar sensation, this double-consciousness, this sense of always looking at one's self through the eyes of others, of measuring one's soul by the tape of a world that looks on in amused contempt and pity. One ever feels his twoness — [...] two souls, two thoughts, two unreconciled strivings; two strivings[.][6]

That message enables the development of a doubled white racial consciousness for Jess. This doubling is not a kind of "me–too–ism" (i.e., white people are also oppressed) but an ability to understand how it is positioned racially outside of its own system of intentions, which are, so liberal humanist white supremacy erroneously tells us, the measure of racism. Whiteness, Jess realizes, is not of his own making even as it is embedded within his gender and sexuality.

These spaces of genderedness (to use a very awkward expression), historian Siobhan Somerville tells us, have been the result of words, categories, and inventions of white sexologists, the very same scientists "discovering" (read: inventing) racial categorizations.[7] These modern classification systems underscore the relationship between power and how that power is produced through the creation of knowledge. None of these systems are outside of power, outside of white supremacy. They are, in fact, doing the work of political power systems through a kind of work—scholarship—which imagines itself outside of "politics."

Even as sexuality, gender, and race have these documented shared histories, the question that begs to be asked is: what has occurred over the intervening years to allow white supremacist logics to construct sexuality, gender, and race as separate points on different compasses? Let's not lose sight of the fact that what informs the self–image of whiteness—whether many white folks know this or not—is the space and privilege marked, not by knowledge, but by unknowingness. Within this logic, race is something that happens only to folks of colour rather than to white people. The emerging field of anti-racist whiteness studies instead suggests that whiteness is itself both a socially constructed race and a race functioning—not despite a lack of awareness of that construction—but as a lack of awareness.

For white FtMs with histories such as mine, that is, deep inside of lesbian culture and feminist practice, this lack of awareness plays out in predictable ways. One of the most frequent critiques I hear about FtMs is the assertion that, by "crossing over this gender divide" (a metaphor I refuse) and transitioning into a world of masculinity by becoming men, FtM transsexual men are now living a kind of privilege not accorded to lesbians or biological women and so betray their feminist sisters. Even Heather Findlay, editor of the American lesbian magazine *Girlfriends*, claims that she goes into mourning when she "loses another lesbian to the other side."[8]

I am troubled by this critique, with its metaphor of crossing over. While I recognize that the presence of masculinity in dyke contexts has been complex, this notion of crossing over only recognizes one singular mode of identity at a time, not multiple modes working simultaneously. This criticism of crossing over where gender represents the single mode of identity, reveals, in part, an occlusion of all of the other ways that power works to privilege subjects through a combination of things like class, race, sexual orientation, physical ability, and gender. If there is only one side that is good, and one side that is bad, then we are back to ways of thinking about identity as made up of one thing only (gender). That's just far too simple.

What I'm beginning to notice is this: when we think we're seeing FtM transsexual male privilege, I suggest that in fact we're seeing race—that is, whiteness— combining with masculinity to create a far more privileged identity than the cross-over critiques seem capable of suggesting. I'm not putting race and gender here into a hierarchy, but I do want to draw our attention to two things: one, we still live in a white supremacy culture that does far more complex work with race and racialization than we know (and here I mean "we" as in white folks); and two, while claiming trans identity may be significant, amongst trans folks there are still significant differences that we need to start acknowledging.

In Debra A. Wilson's brilliant documentary *The Butch Mystique*, when a "woman" of colour transitions into a FtM transgendered space of masculinity, we'd be remiss to suggest that this FtM is transitioning into a privileged gender position in our culture. Within and amongst communities of colour, masculinity may well be a privileged identity, depending, of course, on what kind of masculinity we are talking about (working class men of colour versus middle-class men of colour; gay men of colour versus straight men of colour). But amongst trans men, white trans men have more power than trans men of colour. This is a perfect illustration of what I mean by in–coherence.

The "T" in LGBTQQI is forced to carry differences amongst trans folks themselves, differences which mark the way we are positioned by other facets of our selves relative to power. Instead of assuming commonality or coherence, I suggest we need to actively seek out difference or in–coherence instead, all the more so if we are white. This means, as a start, not assuming or depending upon commonality. Hard as it might be to grapple with, a trans man of colour is still a man of colour living in white supremacy. That may, in some cases, be easier than living as a butch of colour, but both still face open racism and far more hostility than the white FtM or butch, even though that white FtM or butch has less power, sometimes, than non–trans folks. Yes, my privilege as a white man is measured by the degree to which I can work the illusion of fully embodied white masculinity, but it's still whiteness working here. So, if I have more power as a white transsexual man than I had as a transgendered and extremely masculine lesbian, isn't it my whiteness that is articulating power through my gender and not my gender in and of itself?

In our zealousness to sort through issues of butchness versus transness, we must not forget that who we are as racialized subjects makes all the difference in what kinds of questions we need to ask about how our bodies are articulated by systems of power. Not assuming commonality in one's experience of masculinity is a good example. And for me, there's the rub. This is where life looks very different. What I'm far more aware of now than ever before is not just how different my life is because of my gender, but also, how different my life is because of the racialization of my gender (i.e., white man, not just man). In our desires to be recognized and valued in our chosen genders, we still have all the obligations, if not more, of socially conscious white masculinities. To fail in that obligation is to duplicate white supremacy, knowingly or otherwise.

Dudes and Dicks

Besides their history, though, trans and butch do share one thing in common: both are potential examples of non–phallic politicized masculinity, something this simplistic idea of "crossing over" dismisses. FtM surgeries have not advanced to the degree where they can produce sensate, functioning penises. Some surgeons try, although most of the time "bottom surgeries" are never covered by health care (frankly, most of the time neither are chest surgeries in Canada). At the cost of anywhere from $20,000–$70,000, surgically manufactured penises are simply cost prohibitive for most trans guys. Guys are out there living without conventional looking dicks. The trans guys who do self–identify as inbetweens, as men with what some guys are calling bonus holes, provide further evidence that this simplistic notion of FtMs as crossing over into "manhood" cannot hold.

Historically, butches were also equally condemned as too male–identified for many who did not understand the complexities of butch–femme as a sexual system that is different from heterosexuality. The two can look similar, but, in many ways, they are different. For instance, butch–femme is often organized around strong, stone femmes and tough, but also vulnerable, butches; in that, then, sexual pleasure is often focused on the femme's pleasure, not exclusively on the butch's. *Stone Butch Blues*, as an example, documents this turnabout in very interesting ways.

But the difference between butches and FtMs is this: in our culture right now, the measure of a gender is the degree to which that gender is publicly visual and visible. Jamison Green calls this phenomena a cultural agreement; that is, he calls this an unspoken understanding about what counts as a "real" gender. In North America, this is one that visually looks like a "real" gender. As much as I no longer see myself as a butch, for many who are still stuck within either/or ways of thinking, that's exactly what I am, precisely because I don't have a penis. For others, those closest to me and for those with complicated ways of reading nuanced bodies outside of that either/or dichotomy, I'm neither a queer butch nor a straight guy. In this way of thinking, trans masculinity may well be the evolution of butchness into a totally new kind of gender.

The other thing I'm fascinated by in this totally new kind of gender is that sexuality can become far more complex. Granted, as a butch I spent most of my time as stone, having a much harder time bringing my gender, body, and desires together all in the same package in that form. As a former stone butch, now female to male trans boi, one of my most cherished pleasures has been watching shows like *Queer as Folk*. For all of its problems — its depictions of queerness as whiteness is extremely troubling — the one thing that it has done for me is provide counter-heteronormative images of what sexualized masculinity can look like. I continue to consume these images of gay masculinity with a great deal of pleasure but also with ambivalence. Repeatedly, although for fleeting moments, part of what I found myself looking for in each episode, especially those of group sex, or bathhouses, or the back room of Babylon, have been those scenes of male penetration and male bottoming.

One of the complexities of men bottoming — either for other men or for women — is its in-coherency within heteronormativity. One of the things that I find myself drawn to in gay male cultures is its unabashed depiction of top-bottom relationships between men. For Brian and Justin, the choreography of top-bottom plays out literally across age lines. Sexual receptivity — that is, penetration — is often depicted and visualized in gay sex cultures, not as diminishing masculinity, but as positive, as sexy, and as an assertion of sexual power. In "Recasting Receptivity," Ann Cvetkovich similarly reads the narratives of butch–femme and gender queer cultures to suggest that sexual receptivity — what she calls "being fucked" — is an active and engaged process. "Different kinds of penetration mean different things," she argues, providing a way of thinking about bottoming as different from submitting. "One is actively doing the labour of pleasing a sexual partner within agreed upon sexual scenarios, the other is far more passive. As a result, penetration, [functions] as a metaphor that signifies not domination but something else."[9] Receptivity can, then, signify both an openness to one's own pleasure and also a willingness to give someone else pleasure.[10]

This willingness to give someone else pleasure blurs dichotomies between top–bottom, active–passive, male–female, gay–straight, trans/non–trans. Images of gay men provide ways for me to rethink and reorganize sexuality. As a former stone dyke turned boi, I can experience sexual pleasure and power through penetration in this body which, like Cvetkovich notes above about receptivity, is marked as something else, outside of the normalized gender maps. This space of something else — where things do not make sense in the conventional ways of organizing genders, bodies, and pleasures — is a form of in–coherence.

Cultivating a practice of in–coherence is, it seems to me, a necessary adaptation to the very material conditions within which FtMs find their bodies located. Very few FtMs can afford successful lower surgery as most phalloplasties remain cost prohibitive. Many more, like me, do not necessarily desire the procedure. Many of the FtM bodies depicted, for instance, in the photographs of Del La Grace Volcano are trans and in–coherent within current sex/gender economies. These are very different kinds of bodies and narratives, defying "legitimating" narratives about "bodies which betray," narratives that ensure access to sex reassignment hormones and procedures.

My question about living in–coherently, even for those trans men who do have bottom surgery, is this: what happens to what's euphemistically identified quietly amongst FtM men as "the tranny bonus hole"?[11] This is not the same hole that defines femininity. This is the hole that defies these simple categories of penis = male, vagina = female, and so on. This hole does not lead to reproduction nor is it boxed in by its biological capabilities. For me personally, it exists as a way of thinking about the possibilities of embodiment, critical gender practices, and sexual politics outside of the ways that heterosexual men should experience sexual pleasure. Regardless of whether or not trans men have bottom surgery, most of us, if not all, continue to live our lives as men, dare I say it, with boy pussies inconsistent with masculinity. For those of us who are straight with a twist, it takes very sexually adventurous and equally off-the-gender maps (for me: femme top) partners to negotiate through these complex bodies.

From Dyke Daddy to Trans Boi

Through these "transitions," many trans guys refuse definitions of adult hegemonic manhood itself. To refuse power as a white man does not mean disavowing one's positioning within white supremacist grids of power. If a lack of racial consciousness is one of the privileges of power, then such tactics of refusal mean locating oneself precisely within these grids, albeit with a stealth critical practice. There are now more ways of living as a self–conscious, politicized man than ever before. I've given many talks on FtM masculinities and female masculinities in many parts of Canada. One of the most common things I see both in my audience, and in conversation with folks afterward, are the ways that many FtMs are redefining white manhood as they step into it.

Yes, many trans guys date straight women. Just as often, though, many date other trans guys. Or, some trans guys bottom for lesbian femme tops. Or some are into gay men while others might be into MtFs. If trans guys are helping to generate new genders, we are also seeing the construction of new sexual subjectivities for masculinity. And yet our ways of thinking are still very limited to and by the homonormative options of "gay" or "straight." That is, these categories are too normatively singular. While it might seem odd to think of gay as normative, it certainly makes sense if we draw distinctions between "gay" and "queer." These options cannot hold the contradiction that I described earlier: being a straight guy who's half lesbian. Nor can they explain being a queer identified heterosexual man by, amongst other things, bottoming sexually or maintaining the space of F on my official identification papers. I'm interested in troubling the straight ways that masculinity is defined in our culture.

And what about the trans guys who transition into younger male identities? I recently gave a talk at the University of British Columbia in Canada where one young FtM found me during the reception to thank me for putting into words something he'd been trying to articulate for a while. During my talk, I raised a question about the degree to which FtMs often identify with the idea of boyhood instead of manhood. This possibility calls for a recognition and rethinking of biographical ideas of time as much as historical ideas about time. It also challenges homonormativity.

For instance, as a butch, I never would have considered myself a boy. It just wasn't, well, butch enough. I needed to be far more masculine and older than I was to deflect homophobia and aggression. As an FtM who signifies as male, I'm often read as much younger than I actually am; as a butch, even as a much younger butch, I seemed much older than my years. Now, I seem much younger. Some of that may well be developmental. My personality is, in some ways, moving again through youth and adolescence as I adjust to a new space of identity. This is still happening in a body that is older than the personality it carries.

Another adjustment towards in–coherence: I seemed, like many other FtMs who transition around the same age that I did (early 40s), to simultaneously experience menopause and adolescence. That makes me wonder if younger FtMs are finding their way into a new type of masculinity that an older butch or FtM might not. I wonder about the differences between bodies like mine, which have lived for almost 30 years with estrogen before testosterone, compared to bodies living with estrogen for significantly fewer years. The gender that each materializes after "transition" may well look different.

These tensions between how I look (much more boi–ish than my years) and my actual age are relatable to names as yet another example of challenging homonormativity. I go by Bobby, but when people have trouble with that, it's because they often want to refer to me by a less boyish name. So, while I never use the names Bob or Robert, I'm constantly surprised by the number of times I'm called by these names. My refusal to be fully "manned" either in language or in body (Bob or Robert versus Bobby), and my refusal to step into the clearly defined space of M to match my gender presentation, signal the differences between trans experiences and the type of genders made visible after transition. That is, medical and clinical regulations of trans identities required that one transition into very normative categories of heterosexual man or woman in order to qualify for transition procedures. With physicians, surgeons, and other trans friendly medical practitioners willing to provide procedures outside of these regulatory bodies, part of what we are seeing now are many different ways of being a trans person, ways that do not align neatly with strictly defined gender norms.

Perhaps this is a measure more of generational differences rather than gender. For butches 50 years ago there may have been only one way of being mannish. Today, not only have scientific and medical advances made trans possible, but also socio–cultural changes in gender roles have given us many more ways of being masculine than ever before. In some ways, trans guys could be likened to the boys of boy bands: young, sweet, soft with all the promise (and all the best moves) of masculinity without having to be defined by whether one achieves adult manhood or not. This type of masculinity doesn't exist only on FtM bodies. Loads of bio guys are realizing they don't have to do it for Daddy, either.

Of course, boy has a long history as a heavily loaded term carrying racism. As Canadian poet and novelist Dionne Brand reminds us, no language is neutral.[12] Not all boyz, bois, boys, or bwoys share the same relationship to language, to power, and to the right of self–naming—making precision and context specific self–naming all the more critical. Still, the idea of boy-hood persists in many contexts and is something trans folks of many races are reclaiming.

And this is where things can get really queer. Trans is not just the new butch. They can overlap sometimes in and through the same body. But they also, at the same time, can mark a relation with, for lack of a better term, male masculinity. This could be trans as the new guy.

Don't worry; we're not likely to see a new type of queerly gendered buddy show like *Will and Grace* any time soon. (Imagine it; the trans boy Butch and his new best friend, Bubba.) But why not? Thinking about trans as not only the new butch historically but also the new guy—as well as the relationship between all three existing on some bodies, like mine, at exactly the same time—might open up entirely dif-ferent ways of thinking about masculinity as some-thing other than the harbinger of all things bad. Either way, the existence of trans masculinity doesn't have to be an indictment of female masculinity nor of male masculinity, either. They can all be different parts of the same story in this historical moment, knowing that ten years from now these may all func-tion differently again.

For me, trans marks a self–conscious fascination with masculinity that was not possible in the same way as a butch. As a trans guy, I'm far more interested in the men in my world than I ever was as a butch. Perhaps it was their hostility toward me as a butch that made it so hard to hold that fascination. What I now know is that the hostility just isn't there anymore. When it is, it doesn't look the same way. That absence has made for some pretty sweet moments with some men that I never thought possible as a big butch in the 1980s. In turn, almost as if we've come full circle, I send the love back to the butches in my life.

I suppose that's why I cling to the need for thinking through paradoxes: I'm a guy who's half lesbian. Just as Patrick Califia admits of himself, I, too, know way more about the lives of lesbians than any straight man is supposed to. Each of these categories of identity — trans and butch and guy — is supposed to cancel out the other(s) when they appear on the same body. They are certainly not supposed to exist all at exactly the same time, and guys are certainly not supposed to have the proud lesbian history I spoke about earlier.

But they do, and I do, and they all are each true at exactly the same moment. One has been my past, one is my current life and who knows, one might be my future in a way I can't anticipate just yet. That's okay. In this queer world, isn't that as good as it gets?

Notes

1. Audre Lorde, *Sister Outsider: Essays and Speeches* (New York: The Crossing Press, 1984).

2. Radclyffe Hall, *The Well of Loneliness* (New York: Avon Books, 1928).

3. Makeda Silvera, "Man-Royals And Sodomites: Some Thoughts On The Invisibility Of Afro-Caribbean Lesbians, " *Piece of My Heart: A Lesbian of Colour Anthology* (Toronto: Sister Vision, 1991).

4. Gayle Rubin, "Of Catamites and Kings: Reflections on Butch, Gender, and Boundaries," *The Persistent Desire: A Femme-Butch Reader*, ed. Joan Nestle (Boston: Alyson Publications, Inc., 1992) 466-482.

5. Judith Halberstam, *Female Masculinity* (Durham and London: Duke University Press, 1998).

6. Leslie Feinberg, *Stone Butch Blues: A Novel* (Ithaca, New York: Firebrand Books, 1993) 178.

7. Siobhan B. Somerville, *Queering the Color Line: Race and the Invention of Homosexuality in American Culture* (Durham: Duke University Press, 2000).

8. Heather Findlay, "Editorial" *Girlfriends: Lesbian Culture, Politics, and Entertainment* March 2003.

9. Ann Cvetkovich, "Recasting Receptivity: Femme Sexualities," *Lesbian Erotics*, ed. Karla Jay (New York and London: New York University Press, 1995) 136-137.

10. Cvetkovich 134.

11. Colin Thomas, *Beyond the binary: adventures in gender*, 31 July 2005 <http://www.straight.com>.

12. Dionne Brand, *No Language is Neutral* (Toronto: M & S, 1998).

The Point Bears Repeating

Jay Sennett

Bent

Tim'm T. West

Somewhere sandwiched
Between the bully and sissy
There was me
Trying to produce in mirrors
A man I could actually love
And want to keep

Bent
Trading my body
For my shadow
Hoping that one would provide
a respite
from the other's torture

my blackness and invisibility
trading places all the time
I've learned well how to
Beat myself up

I am a quintessential shadow boxer nigga
I am buff and so swole
Angry Blackman beating sissy blackboy
Hands inadequate to jerk myself off

I be Mandingo hung
I be neck or slit wrist bent
I be bittersweet strange fruit
Tasting the bite of my own blood
It is sweet....
Like my father has bent me not to be
Bent.

Purpose of Gender
Jay Sennett

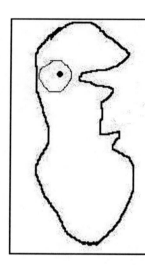

You can use your body to get into your gender. Or, you can use your gender to get into your body. You decide.

www.jaysennett.com/blog

Biographies

Aren Z. Aizura is a writer based in Melbourne, Australia. He's currently completing a Ph.D. on transness and travel and maintains a weblog at http://goingsomewhere.blogsome.com.

White, disabled, and genderqueer, Eli Clare is a poet and essayist with a penchant for rabble–rousing. He has, among other activist pursuits, walked across the United States for peace; coordinated a rape prevention program in Ann Arbor, Michigan; and helped organize the first Queerness and Disability Conference in 2002. Additionally, he has spoken all over the country at conferences, community events, and colleges about disability, LGBT identities, and other social justice issues. Eli is the author of *Exile and Pride: Disability, Queerness, and Liberation* (South End Press, 1999). More recent work can be found in *GLQ: Desiring Disability – Queer Theory Meets Disability*

Studies, From the Inside Out: Radical Gender Transformation, FTM and Beyond, and *Dangerous Families: Queer Writing on Surviving*. He lives in Vermont and works at the University of Vermont's LGBTQA Services. When not otherwise occupied, you can find Eli having fun adventures with his sweetie, riding his trike, and hanging out with his dog.

Gaylourdes was once a secretly passionate pianist. He's a student in Performance Studies and lives in Sydney, Australia. He can be contacted via http://gaylourdes.blogsome.com.

Doran George is an artist, dancer, writer, and curator. His "live art" work has been staged across Europe and the United States and has ranged from him being encased in brick for a working day to having a sexual relationship as an art practice. He has been supported by the London Arts Board; The Arts Council of England; The British Council; Chisenhale Dance Space; Arnolfini, Artsadmin; The Finnish Arts Council; The Arts Council of North Savo (Finland); Stichting Fonds De Trut (The Netherlands); and others. He has curated for "The International Transgender Film Video Festival" (U.K. and The Netherlands), "Vital Signs Festival" (U.K.) — (interfaces between disability politics and contemporary art), and Chisenhale Dance Space. He regularly contributes to symposia and is published in print and on the web in dance, film, and performance art journals and art publications. Doran has a B.A. in experimental dance and choreography and an M.A.

in Feminist Performance. He teaches in universities in the United States, Britain, and Central Europe.

Jordy Jones is a long-time San Francisco resident currently residing part-time in the California High Desert Arts Ghetto of Joshua Tree. He is a scholar, curator, multimedia artist, and community advocate. His work has included the investigation of issues of the human body and its relationship to economics, technology, culture, censorship, and the law. Jones has worked with cultural organizations as diverse as the San Francisco Art Institute; The GLBT Historical Society; The International Lesbian and Gay Association; Los Angeles Contemporary Exhibitions; Intermedia Arts Minnesota; and The Guggenheim Soho, New York. He has served on the governing boards of The San Francisco Pride Celebration and Parade Committee, The Alice B. Toklas LGBT Democratic Club, and The Lab. He is a past member of the LGBT Advisory Committee of the San Francisco Human Rights Commission. As male chair of the San Francisco Transgender Civil Rights Implementation Task Force, he was key in implementing trans inclusion in the health benefits package for city employees and for furthering trainings for the police and sheriff's departments. He has a B.A. in Conceptual and Information Arts, an M.A. in Museum Studies and is pursuing a Ph.D. in Visual Studies and Critical Theory at the University of California, Irvine, where he is a UC Chancellor's Fellow. His dissertation, due for completion in 2008, is entitled *The Ambiguous I: Photography, Gender, Self.* According to Mark Leno, member of the

California State Assembly representing District 13: "Jordy Jones is San Francisco's Secret Weapon!"

At the age of five Nick Kiddle wanted to be a missionary: "I'm still trying to spread the truths I've learned. I studied physics at university because I was lucky enough to have the chance, but writing was always my first love. I've written six Sci-Fi novels, and I'm carving out the seventh page by page, whenever I have a break from the demands of single parenthood."

Bobby Noble (Ph.D., York University) is an Assistant Professor of sexuality and gender studies in the School of Women's Studies at York University (Toronto, Canada). Bobby is the author of the recently published *Sons of the Movement: FtMs Risking Incoherence in a Post-Queer Cultural Landscape* (2006, Toronto: Women's Press) and *Masculinities Without Men?: Female Masculinity in Twentieth Century Fiction* (University of British Columbia Press, Winter 2004) and is co-editor of *The Drag King Anthology*, a 2004 Lambda Literary Finalist (Haworth Press, 2003). Bobby is currently working on a new book project, *Boy Kings: Canada's Drag Kings & Masculinities in Performance*.

Jay Sennett is an author, filmmaker, anthologist, blogger, and publisher; permanently white and temporarily able bodied. In 2006 he founded Homofactus Press, a small publishing company dedicated to culture making by and for FtM communities. He has worked on a variety of films in various capacities since 1990, including writing, directing, shooting, and editing *Phallocy*, a three-minute short screened in over forty film festivals worldwide. His art is driven by his political activism. Indeed, Homofactus Press has grown out of his belief that art must be part of the communities it serves as well as his belief that artists must receive fair royalties for their efforts. He is currently hard at work on his novel *Terror* and two additional books by different authors to be published in 2007. In between writing and editing and marketing, he finds time to draw and post his cartoons at www.jaysennett.com/blog. To learn more about Homofactus Press, visit www.homofactuspress.com.

Scott Turner Schofield began his performance art career working as a research assistant to Holly Hughes and Carmelita Tropicana at New York City's WOW Cafe in 2000. Now a full-time performance artist, educator, and producer, he tours his acclaimed one-trannie shows *Underground Transit, Debutante Balls*, and *Becoming a Man in 127 Easy Steps* around the world. He has only been censored once, but *boy was that a party!* Schofield has been honored with several commissions for new work and is the youngest recipient of a Tanne Foundation Award for Outstanding Achievement and Commitment to Art. He currently lives in Atlanta and will always call the South home.

When Eli J. VandenBerg began transitioning, he also began creating self-portraits. Throughout his transition, he created and continues to create images of what his body looks like in the mirror and what it looks like in his mind. This series, like his body, is work in progress. Eli received his B.F.A in Printmaking from Arcadia University and his M.F.A in Printmaking at Pratt Institute. He now works at The Print Center in Philadelphia. He has shown his work both nationally and internationally and was recently featured in "The National Queer Arts Festival." His works have also appeared in several books and magazines. For more information about Eli and his work, visit www.adventuresinboyhood.com.

Tim'm T. West is an author/publisher, poet, emcee, scholar, and activist who, in 1999, co-founded Deep Dickollective and established himself as one of the more dynamic and influential Renaissance artists coming into the 21st Century. In 2003, he released a critically acclaimed poetic memoir *Red Dirt Revival*, in 2005 a chapbook *BARE*, and will release his second full-length book, *Flirting*, through Red Dirt Publishing. Musically, he released his solo debut, *Songs from Red Dirt*, on Cellular Records. *Blakkboy Blue(s)* was its highly anticipated follow up. *On Some Other* was DDC's third full–studio album project. A cultural critic, Tim'm is widely published in academic and literary anthologies, journals, and other publications.

LaVergne, TN USA
16 September 2010
197340LV00007B/172/A